D1585104

CO-ROMANIA

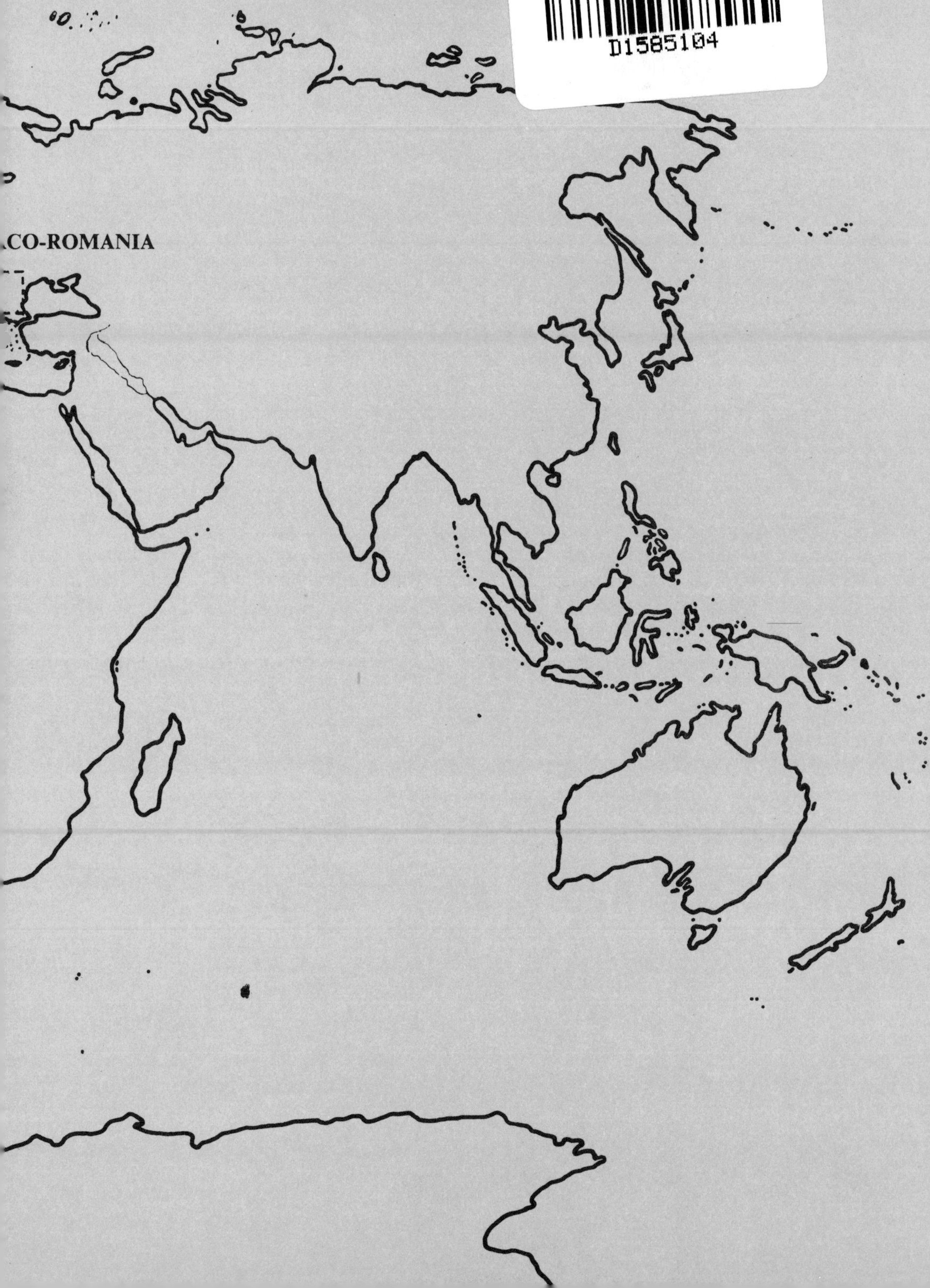

In the same series :

INDOCHINA	Bernard P. Groslier, Curator of Historical Monuments, Angkor ; Director of Archaeological Research, Ecole Française d'Extrême-Orient
INDONESIA	Bernard P. Groslier, Curator of Historical Monuments, Angkor ; Director of Archaeological Research, Ecole Française d'Extrême-Orient
JAPAN	Vadime Elisseeff, Curator at the Cernuschi Museum, Paris
MESOPOTAMIA	Jean-Claude Margueron. Member of the French Institute of Archaeology, Beirut
MEXICO	Jacques Soustelle
PERSIA I (From the origins to the Achaemenids)	Jean-Louis Huot, Member of the French Institute of Archaeology, Beirut
PERSIA II (From the Seleucids to the Sassanids)	Vladimir G. Lukonin, Head of the Oriental Department, Hermitage Museum, Leningrad
PERU	† Rafael Larco Hoyle, Director of the Rafael Larco Herrera Museum, Lima
PREHISTORY	Denise de Sonneville-Bordes, Ph. D.
ROMANIA	Constantin Daicoviciu, Director of the Archaeological Institute of Cluj, and Emil Condurachi, Director of the Archaeological Institute of Bucharest
ROME	Gilbert Picard, Professor at the Sorbonne, Paris
SOUTHERN CAUCASUS	Boris B. Piotrovsky, Director of the Hermitage Museum, Leningrad
SOUTHERN SIBERIA	Mikhail Gryaznov, Professor at the Archaeological Institute, Leningrad
SYRIA-PALESTINE I (Prehistory and Ancient Orient)	Jean Perrot, Head of the French Archaeological Mission in Israel
SYRIA-PALESTINE II (Ancient and Classical Orient)	Aharon Kempinski of the University of Tel Aviv and † Michael Avi-Yonah, Professor at the University of Jerusalem
THAILAND	Pisit Charoenwongsa and C. Subhadradis Diskul, Professor at the Silpakorn University, Bangkok
TRANSHIMALAYA	Giuseppe Tucci, President of the Italian Institute for the Middle and Far East, Rome
URARTU	Boris B. Piotrovsky, Director of the Hermitage Museum, Leningrad

ARCHAEOLOGIA
MVNDI

Series prepared under the direction of Jean Marcadé,
Professor of Archaeology at the University of Bordeaux

To the memory of my brother

IANCU BERCIU

DUMITRU BERCIU

DACO-ROMANIA

With contributions by BUCUR MITREA
(Chapter VII and parts of Chapters II, III and VIII)

65 illustrations in colour ; 73 in black and white

Translated from the French by JAMES HOGARTH

NAGEL PUBLISHERS, GENEVA - PARIS - MUNICH

Colour and black-and-white illustrations by Evelley Laszlo
Drawings by Epure Argeş
Maps by Marin Ionescu

I S B N 2-8263-0720-7

CONTENTS

PREFACE

The present work occupies a rather special position in the
"Archaeologia Mundi" series. There is already a volume on Romania in
the series, it may be said : why add another ? Has not the object of
"Archaeologia Mundi"— to present a survey of the varying aspects of
archaeology throughout the world, bringing out its problems, its methods
and its results — already been achieved in relation to the Carpathian
region ? Is there not a danger of repetition ?

In fact it will be found that the two volumes supplement much more than
they duplicate one another. In the first place, of course, new discoveries
are being made all the time, and the archaeological material now
available is much richer ; but above all the point of view in Professor
Berciu's study is different. The problem which concerns him is the
ethnogenesis of the Romanian people, which developed in parallel with the
formation of the Romanian language : hence the emphasis he puts on the
evidence of unity and continuity, in a land constantly racked by the
passage of migrating peoples. There is an apparent paradox here, and it
is fascinating to compare the different destinies of Daco-Romania and the
neighbouring countries.

For the answers to the questions that arise in this field we must look to
archaeology ; but in this quest we must not confine ourselves within the
historical and geographical framework of the Roman province of Dacia.
The author is convinced of the important part played by the Thracian
substratum in the various ethno-cultural syntheses of later centuries.
Thracian unity in turn gave rise to Geto-Dacian unity ; and Geto-Dacian
culture, through its assimilation of cultural elements from Greece, the
Celtic peoples and Rome, well before the time of Trajan, provides an
explanation of the persistence of Roman culture beyond the chronological
limits of official romanisation. The free Dacians also played their part
in maintaining or obstinately re-establishing down the centuries a local
ethno-cultural unity which, fortified by the adoption of Christianity in its
Latin form, enabled the indigenous inhabitants of Daco-Romania to
remain " masters of the land " (in Nicolae Iorga's striking phrase)
throughout successive waves of invasion by the migrant peoples.

Professor Berciu's thesis is argued with a warmth and a scholarly rigour
which carry conviction ; and there is much food for thought in the theory
of " population nappes " and " centres of polarisation " which he develops
in the course of the discussion.

J.M.

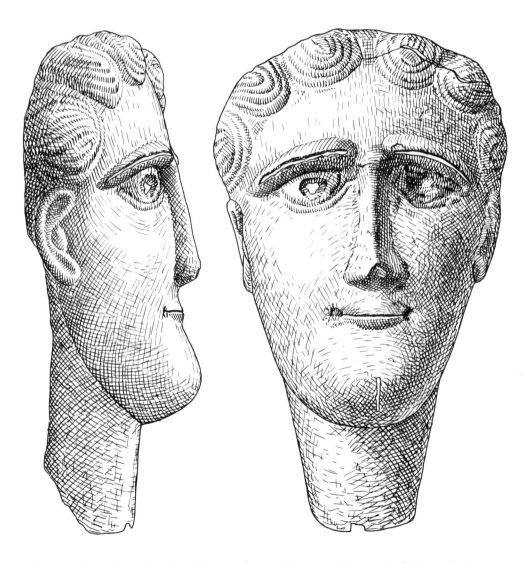

Mask of a divinity in sheet bronze (probably a warlike symbol) from Ocniţa-Ocnele Mari.

INTRODUCTION

It is the object of this study — following the earlier work in the same series by Emil Condurachi and Constantin Daicoviciu, published in 1972 — to trace, in the light of current archaeological knowledge, the history of Romania from the Thracian Bronze Age onwards, paying particular attention to the period from the abandonment of Dacia by the Emperor Aurelian in the 3rd century A.D. to about the 10th century. It was during this period that the Romanian people, that vigorous offshoot of the Eastern Roman world, came into being as a distinct entity. Although the same complex historical process worked itself out in the territory of the Thracians, the Illyrians and other romanised peoples in the Balkans, we shall be principally concerned with Dacia, the country of the Geto-Dacians, which had been so indelibly stamped with the imprint of Rome that it remained " Daco-Roman " during the age of the great migrations when the new ethnic entities of our continent emerged.

Having thus received the mark of Roman culture and firmly established themselves in the Carpatho-Danubian region, the Geto-Dacians developed into the Romanians of today, still inhabiting the land of their ancestors. As the great Romanian historian Nicolae Iorga observed, surveying the whole territory embraced by Eastern Roman culture : " In no part of this area did the Thracians subsequently maintain themselves as such : they survived only in those Romance traditions, with their various adaptations and interpretations, which now became specifically Romanian " (1936). This unity and continuity can be explained only in terms of the prehistoric and proto-historical substratum of Romania ; and accordingly we shall be particularly concerned in this study with certain problems relating to the period before the Roman conquest, in order to identify the factors which promoted the romanisation of the Geto-Dacians.

We shall begin by considering the make-up of the Thracian substratum which was to constitute an element of stability in the Carpatho-Danubio-Balkan region and to provide the starting point for so many later syntheses.

The second chapter will be devoted to Geto-Dacian material and spiritual culture, in an attempt to define its distinctive individuality and explain the part played by the Geto-Dacians — the major ingredient in the formation of the Romanian people — as an intermediary between East and West in the development of our continent.

This culture, extending over the whole territory occupied by the Geto-Dacians, ensured the unity and continuity of an ancient heritage and its transmission down the centuries to become incorporated in the way of life, the language and the folk traditions of the Romanians. It was able to do this in virtue of its fundamental structure, its contacts with neighbouring peoples (the Puchow and Lipitsa cultures), the elements of universality which it owed to Greco-Roman influence, and its survival in Roman Dacia and, even more significantly, among the free Dacians; for it is now well established that the free Dacians played a part in ensuring the maintenance of the Daco-Roman communities which remained in Dacia after the territory was abandoned by the civil and military authorities of the Empire.

The process of romanisation must be conceived dynamically, having regard to its extension in space and time and to its socio-cultural effects. It was a process that began in the 3rd century B.C. with Rome's first conquests in the Balkans and culminated in the formation of an area of Roman culture bounded on the south by the " Jireček line " and extending in the north to the bastion of the Carpathians and the shores of the Black Sea. (The Jireček line was originally drawn by the Czech philologist Konstantin Jireček as the southern boundary of the Romance language zone. As confirmed by the Romanian philologist A. Philippide, it runs from the Adriatic coast to Skoplje and then continues north-east to a point between Pirot and Bela Palanka, ending in the territory of the Greek cities on the Pontic coast).

But this process was not confined to the 160 years of Roman rule : after the province was abandoned Roman influence north of the Danube did not come to an end. Romanisation now continued from within, the highly romanised territory of Dacia Aureliani (in Moesia) providing a source from which the Daco-Roman population could continually draw fresh strength. The presence of the Roman and Romano-Byzantine Empire on the Danube and in the Dobrudja (known in antiquity as Scythia Minor) exerted an influence in the Carpatho-Danubian area which was felt in many fields — political, economic, cultural and religious.

Between the 4th century, or perhaps earlier, and the 10th a factor of major historical significance was the expansion of Christianity in its Latin form to the mass of the population in the romanised Carpatho-Danubian territories. In recent years archaeology has recovered much evidence dating from early Christian times, and this is of particular importance for the light it throws on the Latinity of the populations concerned.

To the archaeologist the culture of these eastern territories of the Roman world presents a diversity of aspects, varying according to their particular historical circumstances, but its fundamental elements are always Roman, or later Romano-Byzantine ; and when these elements were assimilated by migrating alien peoples to form new syntheses they marked a new stage in the evolution of the societies concerned. Daco-Roman civilisation, an integral part of the civilisation of the eastern Roman world as a whole although it also comprehended many features inherited from the Thraco-Dacians, now pursued its development in the pastoral and farming communities of the region, taking on a markedly popular and rural character. Current archaeological work in Romania is concerned with the survival of Daco-Roman traditions, particularly in the pottery, and excavations all over the country have revealed the existence of cultural complexes like those of Bratei-Moreşti (4th-6th centuries), Ipoteşti-Cîndeşti (7th-8th centuries) and Dridu (8th-9th centuries) — the latter two showing a mingling of Roman and Slav elements on a basis which is still Daco-Roman. This demonstrates the continuing rôle of Roman culture in the Carpatho-Danubio-Balkan region no less than in the West — in Italy, Gaul and the Iberian peninsula — where various migrant peoples were likewise assimilated.

Archaeology is also throwing fresh light on the period when the Slavs established themselves in the region. By the 7th century the Daco-Roman population had already become Proto-Romanian, with all the characteristics of a new ethnic entity — an evolving Latin language, a religion of universal and popular character, a pattern of pastoral and farming communities with their skilled craftsmen, a complex and comprehensive rural culture. The arrival of the Slavs did not lead to the extinction of this culture. It took over certain features from the newcomers, who were assimilated by the Proto-Romanian population north of the Danube, while to the south of the river the reverse process took place, the Proto-Romanians being assimilated or broken down into small separate groups by the Slavs. The written sources relating to the Romanians, which begin to appear in the 9th and 10th centuries, have lent themselves to a variety of interpretations, often motivated by political considerations or based on a misunderstanding of the historical realities ; but the evidence now being produced by Romanian archaeology, confirmed by the linguistic and historical evidence, is making it possible to reconsider and to resolve the old problem of Daco-Roman continuity as well as the wider problem of eastern Roman culture as a whole.

Nor is this continuity to be seen only in Roman Dacia itself (Transylvania, the Banat, Oltenia) : it is found also in other parts of Romania to the north-west, south and east of the Carpathians, where excavations have revealed numbers of settlements belonging to the autochthonous Daco-Roman population. Although the Carpathians — always a factor promoting polarisation — undoubtedly offered a refuge for the romanised population at the time of the first migrations, excavation has not confirmed the hypothesis of a general withdrawal into the mountain regions and a subsequent eastward and southward expansion by the Romanians from the mountains towards the Black Sea. Throughout successive phases of its history — Daco-Roman, Proto-Romanian and Romanian — the whole territory of what is now Romania was occupied by its original population, which absorbed new peoples without losing the unity of its culture, its way of life or its language despite all the vicissitudes of history.

A people is neither a physical nor a metaphysical entity : it is the product of its own history, with the geographical setting also playing a significant part. In this sense it can be said that the Romanians are the people of the Carpathians and the lower Danube, never leaving this homeland even during the period of the great migrations.

As the largest population group in the Carpatho-Danubio-Balkan region, the Romanian people was, more than any other, the product of particular geographical conditions which operated over many centuries and were of particular significance in the mediaeval period. We cannot imagine them leaving the land of their ancestors, even though during the period of the migrations there were movements and interpenetrations between the peoples of the eastern Roman world. It is possible that centres of polarisation of the Proto-Romanian population came into being within the territory of Daco-Romania, conditioned by physical and geographical factors, the hills and rivers, the flora and fauna, the agricultural qualities and the mineral wealth of the soil — the whole architecture of the country in all the diversity of its different parts, varied but harmoniously complementing one another. All this fostered the unity and continuity of a settled existence centred for millennia on the Danube valley.

Linguistic research has shown that the Romanian language was formed in the wide area extending from Trajan's province of Dacia, north of the Danube, to the provinces of Thrace and Illyricum in the Balkan peninsula. In the development of the language two separate periods can be distinguished, before and after the Slav penetration into Daco-Romania and the Balkans. In the earlier period the centre of gravity of the eastern

Roman world lay in the area south of the Danube, in which the cities, the market towns and the episcopal sees were situated and on which the Daco-Roman population north of the river was dependent ; in the later period the language was already shot through with Slav elements.

Recent archaeological work in Romania, taken along with the linguistic evidence and the information given in the historical sources, has shown that from the end of the 3rd to the end of the 6th century the Daco-Roman world was within the sphere of influence of the Roman and Romano-Byzantine Empire. The influence of Byzantium was also felt during the period of symbiosis with the Slav peoples, at first through the intermediary of these incomers and from the 10th century onwards, when the Byzantine Empire reached the Danube, directly. Ethnographically the formation of the Romanian people was then complete, and politically it was beginning to assert itself. Its expansion, however, was brought to a halt by the final wave of migrations ; and it was during this period that the foundations of a feudal structure were laid.

Since a country's economic life, and thus the whole of its social life, is strongly influenced by trade and the exchange of both goods and cultural values, much can be learned from a study of the coins found in the territory with which we are concerned, since they can either confirm or invalidate the results of archaeological or historical research on the technology of the period or the relationships of the Carpatho-Danubio-Pontic region with the Mediterranean world. The finds of coins and the evidence of coining bear witness to the continuous nature of these relationships, beginning even before the year 106, and to the high degree of organisation and civilisation attained by the Geto-Dacians.

The accompanying illustrations and maps will, it is hoped, enable the reader to gain a clearer understanding of the material and spiritual culture of the Carpatho-Danubio-Pontic region during the centuries with which this survey is concerned, and will also provide documentary evidence in support of the historical conclusions formulated in it.

16

THE FORMATION OF
THE THRACIAN SUBSTRATUM

I

There exists in south-eastern Europe a common stock of ancient tradi-tions from which all the various peoples now living in the area stemmed during the early mediaeval period. As the great Romanian historian Nicolae Iorga observed, this heritage of many millennia, some aspects of which are coming to the fore again in our own day, creates a bond between these different peoples ; but none of them is so deeply rooted in these traditions, none is linked with them in such unbroken continuity over a period of four thousand years, as the Romanian people, directly descended as it is from the Indo-European source through the intermediary of the Thracian world which extended from the Carpathians and the Danube region into Asia Minor. This ethnic and cultural substratum, defined by a common language and common beliefs, customs and mentalities, all fused with a pre-Indo-European heritage, had itself inherited the cultural achievements of the Neolithic and Eneolithic societies which were the first settled communities in the Carpathian and Balkan region.

FROM THE ORIGINS TO THE END
OF THE THIRD MILLENNIUM B.C.

The territory of Romania is part of the region in which man came into being, for the latest research into the pebble tool culture has shown that man's first appearance on Romanian soil dates back to the time of the earliest hominids, a million years ago. Of particular interest in this connection are the discoveries made in the middle basin of the Olt, in the Argeş valley and recently at Racoviţa (district of Sibiu), also in the Olt basin. Contemplating the long period that has elapsed since man took his first steps, we are led to reflect on the progress made and the treasures accumulated in this area over these many generations.

The most recent archaeological evidence indicates that the human groups which lived in this area during the Upper Palaeolithic and Mesolithic were passing beyond the stage of hunting and primitive nomadism and were soon to enter on a new way of life based on the cultivation of plants and the rearing of domestic animals. They were thus playing their part in laying the first foundations of European civilisation.

The transition from the Mesolithic to the Neolithic in Romania was achieved in the Iron Gates region by the Schela Cladovei culture, named after an occupation site to the west of Turnu Severin, which is also found at Ostrovul Corbului, to the south of that town. Excavations at these two sites in 1965-70 and further work at Ostrovul Corbului in 1973 brought to light implements made from deer's antlers, sometimes perforated to take a handle, which were evidently used in agriculture. The finds were dated by radiocarbon determinations to about 6000 B.C. Pollen analysis revealed the presence of cereals, pointing to a climate of Mediterranean type. The implements recovered were quite different from those used farther east, and the decoration of some items found both in the Romanian part of the Iron Gates region and in the Yugoslav part (the Lepenski Vir complex) makes it possible to identify in this area a cultural centre based on the cultivation of plants but having no relationship to similar developments in the Near East. The impulses which came from here promoted the progressive development of the Neolithic/Eneolithic ethno-cultural entity which is extensively discussed in the volume on " Romania " in this series.

The latest archaeological discoveries have significantly enriched our knowledge of the cultures which developed between 6000 and 2000 B.C. within the territory of Romania and sometimes beyond its boundaries. The archaeological evidence reveals continuous progress during the Neolithic period and the development within the Carpatho-Danubian and Pontic region of cultures of steadily higher material and spiritual content, whose polished stone tools are always differentiated according to their function. The early pottery also shows steady progress in quality, as exemplified by the splendid painted ware. The working of copper, a new feature characteristic of the Late Neolithic (or Eneolithic, as it is now known to archaeologists), opened a new phase, particularly after all the local deposits of copper were worked out and it became necessary to use ore with a lower copper content from Transylvania and later from Oltenia and the Dobrudja. The copper axes are of different types from those of the Near East and Asia Minor, and the craft of copper-working paved the way for the later working of bronze. (Of significance in this respect are the connections with early bronze-working in Serbia).

Throughout the Neolithic period the population of Romania grew. The number of human settlements increased on both sides of the Carpathians and in the Danube valley, both lowland and upland sites being occupied ; and spiritual life developed in step with material progress. The numerous clay, bone or marble statuettes, the decorated pottery, the items of symbolic rather than practical significance and the cemeteries discovered since the second world war all point to the bond which these people felt with the earth and to their practice of agricultural and funerary cults. The Neolithic saw the laying of the foundations for a stable population, a productive economy and a concern with beauty and convenience.

By the Neolithic/Eneolithic period, in spite of the diversity of successive Neolithic cultures, a Carpatho-Danubio-Balkan cultural entity had been formed in south-eastern Europe. Towards the end of the period, about 2000 B.C., the pre-Indo-European stock of the Carpathians and the Danube region had achieved a synthesis through the fusion of many different elements, varying in importance according to their content, their form and their particular manifestation. In this synthesis, however, the decisive factor was a local one — the stage of internal development reached by the various communities.

THE SECOND MILLENNIUM AND THE FIRST HALF OF THE FIRST MILLENNIUM

At the end of the 3rd and the beginning of the 2nd millennium the pace of socio-cultural and linguistic development quickened. This period saw a process of interpenetration between the pre-Indo-European communities of the Carpathian and Danube regions and newcomers from the east, the fusion between the two being promoted by the mobility of these incomers, who enriched the local cultural stock without altering its basic pattern. It was no doubt this process of fusion that brought about certain anthropological mutations around the year 2000. In this period more than at any other time in their history the people of the Carpatho-Danubian region, with influences playing on them from many quarters, were able to select those elements which were new and progressive and graft them on to their own way of life, adapting them to the needs of their farming and stock-rearing communities. Thanks to the establishment of direct connections between Central Europe and the East the first syntheses were formed in the Coţofeni and Glina cultures. However strong the pressures exerted by the ʹpastoral tribes of the northern Pontic region on the social and economic structures of the Neolithic/Eneolithic population, this was only one factor among others, and the changes which now took place in every aspect of life were the result of a whole complex of elements.

During this period of transition the foundations of a system of agriculture based on the use of a wood or antler ploughshare were laid ; the four-wheeled chariot, a vehicle of Oriental origin, came into use ; the domesticated horse made its appearance ; copper-working developed in South-East Europe, Oriental influence making itself felt only in a later period ; and the first bronze objects were made. After the year 2000 the skills of bronze-working became more widely practised, reaching their full flowering with the crystallisation of the Thracian Bronze Age cultures. In certain areas the economy was more distinctively pastoral, though the stock-farmers practised a primitive form of agriculture on a small scale. just as the agricultural tribes did a certain amount of stock-rearing. During this period too the establishment of a patriarchal system began to take concrete form, reflected in the emergence of large patriarchal families within the tribes. The presence of certain tribal communities near deposits of salt (for example at Ocniţa-Ocnele Mari in the district of Vîlcea) shows that these deposits were now being worked ; and by about the middle of the 2nd

20

millennium salt-working had become a regular economic activity and salt was an object of trade between the tribes. The significant development during this period was the establishment, from about 1700-1600 B.C. onwards, of Bronze Age communities in Thrace, following the completion of the process of linguistic Indo-Europeanisation, and the flowering of the splendid cultures named after the type sites of Tei (Bucharest), Coslogeni, Monteoru, Costişa, Verbicioara, Gîrla Mare, Vatina, Pecica, Wietenberg-Sighişoara and Otomani. (See Map B ; " Romania ", pp. 57 ff. ; and the illustrations in the present volume).

Around 1600 B.C., following the progress achieved in many fields and the blending of a variety of external influences into the local traditions — the major feature of the transitional period between the Neolithic and the Bronze Age — the final crystallisation of the Thraco-Carpatho-Balkan peoples took place. Some of the Thracian tribes moved into Asia Minor, and links were thus established with cultural centres in that area. One of the most significant results of the earlier historical development was the formation of the Thracian Bronze Age substratum, which was destined to become the ethnic and cultural basis for the rise of the Geto-Dacians. Economic and cultural links were established with the brilliant Mycenaean civilisation, bringing into operation the Mediterranean factor which was to accelerate the pace of local development by putting the Thracians into contact with a superior culture.

The Bronze Age saw the establishment of a unified material and spiritual culture and the emergence among the Thracians of traditions which were to survive into later periods. Pottery decoration became increasingly geometric, and some of the decorative themes, like the so-called " sacred fire" patterns, are still found in the Romanian folk art of Transylvania. Over a period of a thousand years Thracian craftsmen, particularly in Transylvania but also outside the Carpathians (for example in the Dobrudja), produced splendid weapons, implements serving a variety of purposes, ornaments, harness trappings, etc., some of which are genuine works of art.   The decoration of some of the swords and battle-axes made in Thrace — in spiral patterns and other designs which were also used in the decoration of pottery — provides clear evidence of the continuity of population in the region, persisting into the first phase of the Iron Age which began about 1000 B.C.   (As we shall see, however, the first iron objects came in from outside Romania).

In the 12th and 11th centuries the Thracian workshops in Transylvania, whose products were distributed throughout the territory occupied by Thracian tribes or tribal groups, provided a link between the various peoples on either side of the Carpathians and the Danube, centred on the ancient Thracian homeland in Transylvania.   A Cluj scholar has recently shown (Rusu, 1972) that the workshops of Transylvania alone had an output of more than 20,000 bronze objects, a much higher figure than the number produced in Central Europe during the same period.

The bronze-working of the Thracians of the Carpatho-Pontic region — who had achieved a major technological advance as a result both of local experiment over a long period and of the assimilation of practices transmitted from the Mediterranean area and Asia Minor — is the most striking demonstration of a natural process of transition from the Thracian Bronze Age to the first Iron Age, which in this area is also ethnically Thracian.   The development of pottery, the conservatism shown in the fortification of settlement or refuge sites and the considerable number of sites, with the demographic implications which this carries with it, all go to show that the Thracians who now entered the Iron Age were not starting from scratch but were continuing a tradition, a culture, a heritage from the past, developing it and carrying it forward in new historical conditions.

As has recently been demonstrated (László, 1974), iron and iron-working appeared at the very climax of the Transylvanian Bronze Age, in the 12th and 11th centuries B.C.   Iron — whose revolutionary rôle in the history of mankind was noted by Friedrich Engels — was at first acquired in the way of trade ; the technique for obtaining it by the reduction of iron ore came later. According to László the first iron objects were brought in from north-east and east of the Alps, material from this area having been identified at Susani (district of Timiş) in the Banat and Lăpuş (district of Maramureş). The working of iron ore and the reduction of the ore to produce iron are first attested within Romania at the beginning of the Hallstatt period, representing an enrichment of the Thracian heritage and a direct prelude to the rise of Geto-Dacian culture. This first phase of the Hallstatt period (the beginning of which, conventionally 1000 B.C., is now dated by archaeological evidence to shortly after 1200) has yielded implements, weapons, ornaments and iron ingots.

By the middle of the 1st millennium the Thracian tribes and tribal groups within the extensive Carpatho-Danubio-Balkan region had strengthened their trading links with the Mediterranean world, central and eastern Europe and Asia Minor, and Greek influence was also beginning to make itself felt, varying in degree between one tribe and another. In spite of these external contacts, however, the Thracian substratum maintained its ethnic unity and homogeneous socio-cultural structure. The maintenance of this unity within such diversity, which can be followed archaeologically from about 2000 to around 600-500 B.C., was due to the capacity for creation, synthesis and assimilation shown by the Thracians, who were thus able to preserve the distinctive individuality of their culture over a wide area extending from north of the Carpathians to the Rhodope range. This substratum formed the basis of the culture of the southern and northern Thracians, whose regional particularisms can also be attributed to the old Thracian heritage from the Bronze Age and the Hallstatt period. The history of many ancient peoples shows that the pace of development can vary within a particular region as a result of internal causes, external influences and other historical circumstances, and also of physical and geographical factors and varying degrees of efficiency in the use of local natural resources ; and this phenomenon can be observed in the Thracian world in the new age which began for the Geto-Dacians about 500 B.C. The differences which can be detected between one area and another, however, in no way affected the old Thracian unity — more specifically Thraco-Geto-Dacian unity — but rather served to give freshness and originality to the culture of this region in the pre-Roman period.

THE GETO-DACIANS
BEFORE THE ROMAN CONQUEST

II

There was a time when European historians did not recognise the Geto-Dacians as being of Thracian stock. Then W. Tomaschek identified the Carpathians as the original homeland of the Thracians, and G. Tocilescu noted in his *Dacia before the Roman Conquest* (1880) : " The Getae and Dacians were neither Germans nor Slavs nor Celts, but Thracians by origin ". Nicolae Iorga was subsequently able to demonstrate the unity of all the Thracian peoples of south-eastern Europe and the Carpathians, a unity founded on a community of language, culture and customs, and thus confirmed the theory of substrata formulated by B.P. Hasdeu.

This old Thracian stock, whose characteristics and considerable achievements have become better known to us through the large-scale development of archaeological excavation and research during the last thirty years, formed the basis on which the Geto-Dacian La Tène culture came into being. In the 5th and 4th centuries the Thracian tribes who lived to the south and east of the Carpathians and on both banks of the lower Danube, known from the time of Herodotus onwards under the generic name of Getae, became involved by degrees in the La Tène culture, following the establishment of indigenous tribal communities which had economic and cultural links with the Greek Pontic colonies of Histria, Tomis and Callatis. As in the case of the Celts, one manifestation of the new phase was the emergence of a " princely " art.

THRACO-GETIC ART

The Thraco-Getic animal style forms part of a larger stylistic unity — a style which flourished between the 5th and 3rd centuries B.C. and which, though produced by many different peoples, showed common features over a very wide area, covering China, Siberia, the whole of the Persian Empire, the steppes north of the Black Sea and the Carpatho-Danubio-Balkan region as far as the Rhodope Mountains and Central Europe, with a particularly rich flowering in Hungary. There was also a Phrygian animal

25

style. This stylistic unity, stemming from different traditions, was expressed in a variety of techniques and themes, related to each people's historical and cultural horizon, the use made of local natural resources and the local way of life, type of organisation and social stratification. Thus in Thracian territory we find a vigorous native element based on a predominantly geometric tradition, which in the La Tène period blended with floral, zoomorphic and other natural motifs to form a new and distinctive organic whole. In the various societies for which objects in the animal style were made the style occupied varying positions in the social hierarchy and was based on different fundamental beliefs — again reflecting diverse ethnic origins. In Persia, for example, it was a " court " style, but in Thrace it was never of comparable status, even among the Odrysae — though the richest hoards and grave deposits belonged to an aristocratic elite which played an important and complex part in Thracian society.

The Getae, who formed a large cultural, social and military entity within the Thracian bloc in the region between the Carpathians, the Balkans and the Black Sea, created an authentic " princely " art, but this was in no sense à court art, the development of which depends on the existence of a well organised state. A brilliant court art — one of the characteristic features of the La Tène culture which grew up on the basis of ancient Thracian traditions — was, however, created in the 4th and 3rd centuries by the Thraco-Getae, living on the confines of the classical world and in proximity to the Scythian art which flourished in the steppes north of the Black Sea. Between these two peoples there were interpenetrations and mutual influences, reflected in the art objects they produced ; but Thraco-Getic art preserved its distinctive originality, as is demonstrated by the illustrations in this book, and even more amply by the treasures displayed in the Romanian Historical Museum in Bucharest and the Thraco-Getic material found in northern Bulgaria. The establishment of relations with the Greek colonies in the Pontic region contributed to the emergence of this art : following these Greek examples, the local aristocracy had learned to assimilate

Mediterranean culture and to enjoy a luxurious standard of life reflecting the hierarchical character of Thraco-Getic society. The influence of Achaemenid Persia is also discernible in the art of the Thracians, most notably in Thraco-Getic art, from which the art of the Carpatho-Danubian region in the subsequent Geto-Dacian and Daco-Getic periods took its origin.

The characteristic features of the Thraco-Getic animal style, mingling traditional decorative motifs of geometric type with figured representations, are known to us either from hoards of valuable objects, like the one found at Băiceni in the district of Iaşi *(Plate 44)*, or from isolated casual finds, like the gold helmet from Poiana-Coţofeneşti in the district of Prahova *(Plate 25)*, or burials, like the chariot burial of a warrior wearing a silver " helmet " found at Peretu in the district of Teleorman.   In 1972 another burial, the tomb of a Getic warrior wearing a bronze helmet of Greek type, was excavated in the village of Găvani (commune of Gemenele, district of Brăila). The tomb also yielded applied ornaments *(Plate 41)* comparable with those found in the rich princely burial in the " Kotys " tomb at Agighiol (district of Tulcea) *(Plate 45)*, dating from the first half of the 4th century.

At Agighiol the excavators found, in addition to the burial chambers of a member of the princely aristocracy and his wife, a stone enclosure in which three of the dead prince's horses had been buried after being killed with poisoned arrows.   The so-called " treasure " of Craiova (in reality a tomb deposit of silver horse trappings), which until 1956 was thought to be Scythian, is now accepted as Thraco-Getic work, a category represented by numerous finds in Romania and Bulgaria *(Plate 38)*.   The bronze emblem sword from Medgidia is also, in the present author's opinion, a work of Thraco-Getic art, but it dates from the 5th century and is strongly influenced by Achaemenid art.   This can be explained by the presence of the Persians in the Balkans following Darius's expedition against the Scythians in 514 : Herodotus notes in his *History* that only the Getae, " the noblest as well as the most just of all the Thracian tribes ", offered any resistance to the Great King. The Thracian and Thraco-Getic aristocracy would thus have an opportunity to see something of the sumptuous way of life of the Persian nobility and the products of Asiatic toreutic art. Like the trading contacts with the Greeks, this glimpse of Persian magnificence helped to give local aristocrats a taste for luxury and for artistic objects. Evidence of this taste is provided by the rich furnishings of tombs, the hoards of gold and silver objects, the use of silver plate (like that found at Agighiol) at banquets, the presence of Greek pottery of the finest quality and the practice of seasoning drinks — particularly Greek wines — with spices, which is attested for example by the strainer found at Peretu. This luxury and ostentation bears witness to the important social, political, military and religious rôle of the aristocracy, who were able to maintain their position until the conquest of Dacia, as is shown by the Dacian fortress (No. 1) at Ocniţa-Ocnele Mari in the southern Sub-Carpathians.

The examples cited show that Thraco-Getic art extended over Oltenia, Muntenia (cf. also the Fîntînele tomb and the 4th century cultural horizon at Zimnicea) and Moldavia (with the gold objects recently found at Stînceşti, in the district of Botoşani, extending its area of diffusion into the northern part of the province). The Dobrudja also falls within the territory of Thraco-Getic art ; and even south-eastern Transylvania has yielded items in the animal style which bear witness to the ethnic and socio-cultural unity of the Getae and the Dacians. Thus the study of Thraco-Getic art of the La Tène period readily reveals the importance of the old indigenous traditions as well as the various outside influences which played their part in the formation of the style.

The appearance of the animal style marked a culminating point in the development of the various Thracian tribes living between the Carpathians and the Rhodope Mountains. It is characterised by the association of animal motifs, reflecting ancient traditions, with figurative or vegetable motifs ; by a strong decorative sense, manifested in a tendency towards abstraction, stylisation and the breaking up of the different parts of a figured representation ; by the use of frames or bands of incised lines as borders to the decorated areas ; and by a controlled dynamism in the use of curvilinear motifs (spirals, volutes, rosettes with three or four arms). From this period dates the introduction of the main themes used by Dacian art in its heyday — some of them, indeed, still found in the Romanian folk art of the present day.

Although some of the figured representations have their origins in the Near East, particularly in Asia Minor and Iran, the bulk of the iconography is characteristically Thraco-Getic, reflecting the local mythology. We are unable to interpret the symbols used in this art — the eagle holding a fish in its talons or a snake in its beak, the bear cub which features in the applied ornaments, the wild boar, the animals with hanging paws, the beasts of prey, etc. To understand them we need to know more about the mythology and religion of the Geto-Dacians, in which we find beliefs inherited from the ancient Thracian substratum, some of them still surviving into our own day, like the snake as a fertility symbol, which can be identified with the " house snake " of Romanian folk tradition. Items of personal adornment like the gold and silver helmets and tiaras and the applied ornaments had a magical function originally linked with the sacred character of the hero, and in the military democracy of the Geto-Dacians this function was transferred to the members of the aristocracy ; for the military leader of the tribal unit not only held political and military power but also performed sacrificial acts of religious significance. The aristocratic elite maintained this dominant position in Geto-Dacian society throughout the history of Dacia down to the Roman conquest ; and the multiplicity of their functions, of which we are informed by the ancient sources, is confirmed by the material recovered from the fortresses of the rulers of this period, like the recent finds at Ocnița (Ocnele Mari).

ECONOMIC RELATIONSHIPS OF THE GETO-DACIANS :
THE EVIDENCE OF COINS

The foundation of the Greek Black Sea colonies (Histria, Tomis, Callatis) in the 7th and 6th centuries B.C. had considerable repercussions on the economic and social life of the Geto-Dacians — affecting in the first place the Getae of the Dobrudja but soon extending to all the Geto-Dacian tribes in the Carpatho-Danubian region. The way for the later romanisation of the population was prepared in advance by their assimilation of many elements of the material and spiritual culture of the Greeks.

Among these elements it is worth considering in more detail the currency used in the trade between the Greeks and the Geto-Dacians. At the outset bronze arrowheads, apparently made at Histria, were used as a means of exchange ; then in the middle of the 5th century Histria began to mint coins with two linked heads on the obverse and a sea eagle devouring a dolphin on the reverse — a type which persisted for eight centuries, as long as the local coinage lasted. These coins, weighing between 4 and 8.4 grammes, were issued in three denominations — drachma, didrachma and stater. The silver coinage was supplemented by bronze coins, originally cast but later stamped, in a variety of types, with a representation of a four-spoked wheel (probably a solar symbol familiar to the local population) and effigies of the river god Istros, Apollo, Dionysos, Demeter, Apollo on the Omphalos, Hermes, etc. The finds of Histrian coins, either in hoards or in isolated examples, cover a very wide area round the Black Sea, not only in Romania but in Bulgaria and the Soviet Union, along the Danube from its mouth to the Iron Gates and inland throughout Geto-Dacian territory. The occurrence of these coins shows that the Geto-Dacians had accepted the use of money as a means of exchange. Histria thus pioneered the use of coins for the purposes of trade in Scythia Minor as Massalia did in Gaul ; and the other Greek colonies of Callatis and Tomis later intensified their coining of money as they developed trading links with the Geto-Dacians of the Carpatho-Danubian region — the former in the 4th and 3rd centuries, the latter in the 2nd century B.C.

Although the coins of Histria were widely diffused throughout Dacia they were not imitated by the native peoples, as a result of the extension of Macedonian authority to the territories round the mouths of the Danube. The occupation of the Dobrudja by Philip II had a detrimental effect on the commercial activity of the Histrians, and the city's coinage was displaced by that of Macedonia, which thereafter steadily increased its influence over the native peoples.

After a period of initiation into the practice of trade based on the use of money the Geto-Dacians began to strike their own coins. This phase represented a process of acculturation, involving the assimilation of a major element of Mediterranean civilisation. The coins were modelled on the tetradrachms of Philip II, the drachmas and tetradrachms of Alexander the Great and the tetradrachms of Philip III Arrhidaios. Beginning in the first half of the 3rd century, the production of Geto-Dacian coins had developed on a considerable scale by the middle of the century, when mints were at work throughout the territory occupied by the Geto-Dacians.

On the basis of differences in technique as compared with the originals, the addition of particular features, some of them of Celtic origin, and the use of particular symbols and devices it is possible to distinguish a number of regional types, which are known by the name of the place where the type was identified or the area where it was discovered. Thus we have the competently produced coins of the type named after Rasa in the Danube valley, modelled on the tetradrachms of Philip II, and the Banat type, with local variants incorporating figurative elements (a bird or dog on the reverse, along with the usual horseman). Another distinctive type is the Tulghieş-Mireşu Mare type characteristic of northern Romania, with a variety of decorative elements — a boar, a shield, various devices, a bow, a rosette, horizontal lines like Roman numerals, a branch underneath the horse. Sometimes the horseman is replaced by a lyre-shaped flower, and the figure of Zeus on the obverse by a likeness of Apollo. These coins, like the coins of Moldavia (the Huşi-Voosieşti type), show a number of Celtic features, and this has led some scholars to suppose that the Celto-Bastarnian tribes minted coins in Moldavia. The problem is, however, a very complex one, and we are still not sufficiently informed about the part played by the native Geto-Dacian population of Moldavia in the production and use of this new means of exchange. With their close links with the Greek colonies, the Geto-Dacians of the Dobrudja did not feel any need to imitate the coinage of Macedonia, since they were able to use Greek coins for the purpose of commerce and trade. There were, however, some leaders of tribal groups, both Getic and Scythian, who struck their own coins : for example the didrachma of the Moskon type found in the northern and north-western Dobrudja.

The second stage in the development of Geto-Dacian coin production began in the middle of the 2nd century. The general lines of the earlier type were maintained, but stylisation was carried to a point where the representation of the original model became purely schematic. The fineness of the silver was steadily reduced and the copper content increased, and the coins weighed only half as much as before. During this phase a number of types can be distinguished by the degree of stylisation of the Macedonian tetradrachm and the use of different symbols or devices. Sometimes the head of Zeus and the horseman on the reverse dissolves into a pattern of blobs, and the coins may take on a concavo-convex shape.

In addition to the coins minted by the colonies on the west coast of the Black Sea, the coinage of Macedonia and the native coins which can be assigned to various Geto-Dacian tribes, there were in circulation also drachmas and tetradrachms from Thasos, Macedonia Prima and the two Greek colonies of Dyrrachium and Apollonia on the Illyrian shores of the Adriatic. These coins circulated in large numbers all over Geto-Dacian

4

5

6

7

8

9

10

11

12

13

14

15

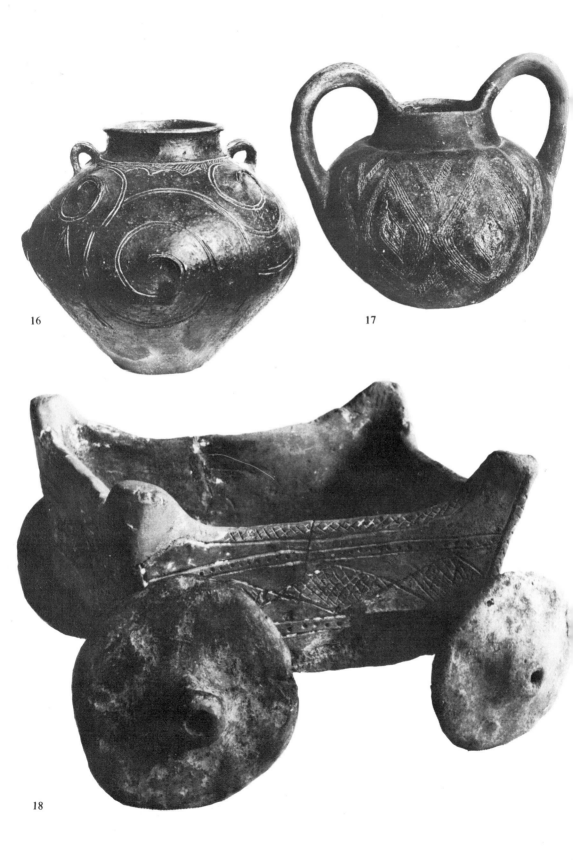

16

17

18

territory, and some of them were imitated by the native peoples. Up to 1969 a total of 450 drachmas from Macedonia Prima and 2900 from Thasos had been found either in hoards or in isolated examples, and subsequent finds have increased these figures by several hundreds.

The coins belonging to the second group, distributed throughout Albania, Yugoslavia and western Bulgaria, with Romania as their farthest point, were found in hoards, either by themselves or in association with Roman denarii of the Republican period, and thus provided evidence of trading links between the Geto-Dacian tribes and these distant cities in the 2nd century B.C., when economic relations with Rome were becoming increasingly close. The study of distribution maps has made it possible to establish that the gold coin known as the *KOSON* type, after the legend in Greek letters on the obverse, with effigies on both sides copied from Roman denarii, is found only in Daco-Getic territory and must therefore be of Geto-Dacian minting. But during the 1st century, in the time of Burebista, when the tendency towards the unification of the Geto-Dacian tribes was actively at work, the local coins gave place to the Republican denarius, of which no fewer than 26,000 have been found, either in hoards (228) or in individual examples. The historical significance of this figure can be appreciated if we remember that the corresponding total for Illyricum, within the territory of present-day Yugoslavia, is of the order of a few dozen, for Pannonia around ten and for the area south of the Danube something like fifty.

Archaeologists were long puzzled by the occurrence in Dacia of this disproportionately high number of Roman denarii dating from the last century of the Republic, but the explanation has at last been suggested by the recent discovery in a Dacian fortress at Tilişca, near the town of Sibiu, of more than ten dies reproducing with considerable fidelity both the obverse and reverse of Roman denarii of the first half of the 1st century : this was evidently a local mint for the production of Roman coins. On other sites moulds or traces of casting, coin blanks, etc., have been found. A recent study by the present author of the huge mass of Republican denarii found in Dacia has made it possible to distinguish those which can be attributed to Dacian mints. The main features pointing to local Dacian minting are clumsiness of execution in comparison with the output of the Roman mints, partial or superficial impression of the effigies, lower silver content, difference in weight, imperfect reproduction of the legend, the size of the blank, etc. There still remain, however, a considerable number of genuine Roman coins, no doubt brought by Roman merchants travelling to Dacia on business, two centuries before Trajan's conquest. This indicates the advanced stage reached by the Dacians in the development of trade : in accepting this money, a currency which circulated among the civilised peoples within the orbit of Rome, the Dacians were becoming involved in the European economy of the period. They had thus entered a new phase in their socio-economic development : a phase marked also by the increased importance of craftsmen and, even more significantly, of the native businessmen, who were to become the most active agents and the beneficiaries of romanisation in Trajan's province of Dacia. Evidence of this is provided by the inscription PETR, in Latin characters, incised with a pointed instrument on a denarius in a hoard recently discovered at Cetățeni (district of Argeș). The inscription very probably represents the name of a local businessman who dealt with Roman merchants. The rise of this new merchant class heralded the end of the power of the Geto-Dacian aristocracy, a power founded on religious beliefs dating from the period of formation of the Indo-European peoples.

CONTACTS AND ASSIMILATIONS, SYNTHESIS AND PROGRESS

In addition to the two factors already mentioned — the appearance of a new style of art and the move towards the use of money as a medium of trade — the European culture known as La Tène, and with it the culture of the Geto-Dacians, was characterised by the introduction of the potter's wheel, which

242

transformed the making of pottery from a domestic craft into a true skilled craft practised by specialised craftsmen in their own workshops. Even after the introduction of the wheel, however, pottery continued to be made by hand. The spread of the wheel began in the region lying between the Danube and the sea, and the main effect of the new technique was felt along the Danube valley, beginning in the plains of Muntenia, Oltenia and Moldavia and then extending into the hilly region and the Sub-Carpathians. By the 5th century the wheel had come into use throughout the Pontic and extra-Carpathian regions, and in the 4th century it became the normal technique. In the Carpatho-Danubian (Thracian and Pontic) region wheel-thrown ware is found sporadically from the late 6th and early 5th century. The use of the wheel was introduced to the Getae through the intermediary of the Greeks, with the impetus coming from the peoples of southern Thrace.

Using the wheel, local potters produced vases imitating Greek prototypes like the oinochoe, with a raised handle and a three-lobed spout — a type which the native potters also made by hand. As an example we may take a vase from Ostrovul Mare, in grey fabric, dating from the early La Tène period. A second group of wheel-turned vases characteristic of the Geto-Dacian La Tène show a traditional form reflecting ancient Thracian traditions. Later in the period the Geto-Dacian potters imitated, but always in a distinctively indigenous style, other forms — Hellenistic, Hellenistico-Roman and finally, at the end of the lst century B.C., Roman. The spread of the potter's wheel and the appearance of fine ware of Geto-Dacian La Tène type are phenomena which can be observed throughout the whole of the Thraco-Getic region, including the Getic territory east of the Carpathians.

Excavations carried out in Moldavia in recent years have yielded imported Greek pottery, particularly amphoras from Chios and Thasos, but also locally made wheel-turned ware. The Getae of north-eastern Romania reached the La Tène cultural level at about the same time as those in the lower Danube valley, although the pace of social and economic development was slower in the areas farther from the centres of Greek civilisation in the western Pontic region and from the zone of Macedonian or Thraco-Odrysian influence. The material recovered between the eastern Carpathians and the river Prut and in the Danubio-Pontic region shows the same continuity and specifically indigenous creation. The investigation of fortresses and settlements at Stînceşti, Cotnari, Moşna and many other Getic sites has shown that by the 4th century La Tène culture had reached the Getae of north-eastern Romania, the evidence for this conclusion being provided by a study of the pottery, both wheel-turned and hand-made. This La Tène culture developed out of the local Hallstatt culture, itself the vigorous continuation of a distinctive indigenous tradition.

The La Tène culture of the region east of the Carpathians was notable in the 4th century not only for its wheel-turned pottery but also for its Thraco-Getic " princely " art. We have already had occasion to refer to the hoard of gold objects dating from the 4th century which was found at Băiceni, pointing to the existence of a Getic aristocracy in this part of Romania. On the evidence of the pottery, however, the earliest La Tène period among the Geto-Dacians shows no signs of Celtic influence : as archaeological investigation has demonstrated, this began to make itself felt at a later stage in the lower Danube region, for example at Zimnicea.

THE NATIVE PEOPLES, THE CELTS AND
THE BASTARNAE

In western and north-western Daco-Romania the Celts were destined to play a part of some significance in the socio-economic development of the native peoples and in the enrichment of the Geto-Dacian cultural heritage, on which the Roman contribution was later to be grafted. Recent archaeological results (e.g. the material recovered in the Fîntînele cemetery, in the district of Bistriţa-Năsăud, and the excavations at Aradul Nou) have indicated that Celtic penetration into western Romania began in the first half of the 4th century, and that after a number of violent clashes the indigenous peoples and the incomers reached a *modus vivendi* enabling them to live side by side. The presence of the Celts until about the middle of the 2nd century is firmly established by archaeological evidence.

There was no question of Celtic domination of the Dacians : so far no Celtic oppida, of the type found in Central Europe, have been identified in Romania. But it was the Celts who gave the impulse for the crystallisation of the Geto-Dacian La Tène, both in the plains of western Romania and in the intra-Carpathian zone, by contributing to the creation of a unified and enriched La Tène culture of indigenous character. Through their agency the use of the potter's wheel was widely diffused throughout Dacian territory and new metal-working skills were introduced. It should be recalled, however, that the Thraco-Dacians had been working local deposits of iron ore since the 12th century, extracting the metal by a reduction process : when the Celts arrived, therefore, there was already a long established tradition of metal-working.

Celtic influence also made itself felt on the Getae living to the south and east of the Carpathians, in the production of wheel-turned pottery, the working of iron and the manufacture of a whole series of items of adornment. In the local painted pottery as well as in local architecture Celtic features are discernible alongside the predominant Hellenistic elements. As we have already seen, too, Celtic influence is also evident in some types of Geto-Dacian coins. Recently two hoards of iron objects found in Moldavia (commune of Negri, district of Bacău ; commune of Oniceni, district of Neamţ) have been shown to be of Celtic origin, and material of Celtic workmanship has also been found in the lower Danube region.

What concerns us here, in relation to the material presented in the earlier volume on " Romania ", is the contribution made by the Celts and other peoples who came into contact with the indigenous population in the protohistorical period and during the lst millennium and were finally assimilated by that population, stimulating and enriching their culture in varying degrees. It is important to note, however, that this was not a one-way traffic and that the Celts themselves received influences from the Geto-Dacians. This has been demonstrated by recent archaeological work, which has shown that as a result of constant economic and cultural exchanges across the Carpathians the Celts in Transylvania played a part in the diffusion and wider adoption of certain cultural features which originated among the Getae of the extra-Carpathian and Pontic regions : for example certain items of personal adornment like the knobbed bracelets of Thraco-Getic type, the fibulas of Thracian type and characteristic Geto-Dacian pottery types like the biconical jug with a raised handle or the handled cup of Thracian origin which is also found in the Illyrian world. Thracian and Thraco-Getic features have also been detected in the Celtic pottery of Transylvania. A two-way exchange of influences can likewise be seen in the field of military equipment, for example in the ornamentation of harness trappings.

Thus Romanian archaeological research has demonstrated clearly that the native peoples exerted an influence on the Celts, giving their La Tène culture a distinctively different character from the corresponding Celtic culture in Central and Western Europe. The existence of a Thraco-Getic La Tène culture in the extra-Carpathian and Pontic regions before the arrival of the Celts led to the development of mutual contacts and exchanges between the two La Tène cultures. It is now also generally accepted that it was the presence of the Thraco-Getic tribes that prevented the Celts from sweeping on towards the western coast of the Black Sea. Moreover, recalling Vasile Pârvan's view that the Celts facilitated the process of romanisation, we may observe that as a result of prolonged contacts between the two peoples — usually hostile, more rarely peaceful — they both shared in the cultural advances which the Celts diffused throughout pre-Roman Dacia in different forms and at different times. These factors, following on the influence exerted over a long period by the Greeks, contributed to the establishment in the Danube and Carpathian region of a pattern of classical Greco-Roman civilisation which prepared the ground for the advance to a higher cultural level after the Roman conquest.

In addition to these various constituent elements, all well attested by archaeological evidence, mention must also be made of the Scythian influence from Transylvania which preceded the arrival of the Celts. This Scythian influence, however, did not represent a stimulus in the advance towards the new Iron Age : rather it was a retarding influence calculated to perpetuate the pattern of the late Hallstatt period. Nevertheless it can be said that the association of Scythian and Thracian elements contributed to the formation of the Celtic style of the early La Tène period in Central Europe.

Towards the end of the 3rd century B.C. a Germanic tribe, the Bastarnae, made their way into eastern Romania. They found the indigenous Getic population in possession of a culture which already showed the characteristics of La Tène, though certain features of that culture still reflected survivals from an earlier period. The Bastarnae were themselves at the La Tène stage, and thus contributed nothing to the development of the local La Tène culture. Settling in the area between the Carpathians and the Dniester, the Bastarnae co-existed with the Geto-Dacians until the middle of the lst century B.C. (the time of Burebista), forming a cultural group characterised by its pottery, known as Poieneşti ware. This pottery spread throughout the eastern part of Daco-Romania, where it was associated with the Lukashevka culture. The Poieneşti-Lukashevka complex is properly to be regarded as a Bastarnian cultural entity in Geto-Dacian territory, destined in due course to be assimilated by Geto-Dacian culture. The most recent archaeological work has made it possible to define more exactly the area of diffusion of this cultural complex and has discredited the statements in the written sources that the Bastarnae moved down into the Danube delta. The archaeological map shows no signs of

Bastarnian material south of a line running through Piatra Neamţ, Roman and Tiraspol. The Getic fortified settlements *(davae)* to the south and south-west survived, while those to the north (Stînceşti, Cotnari) were apparently destroyed by the Bastarnae. It has also been established that the Bastarnae used Geto-Dacian pottery, which has been found on Bastarnian sites at Botoşana, Lunca Ciurei, Tîrpeşti and elsewhere.

Thus in the 2nd and 1st centuries B.C. the whole of north-eastern Romania formed part of a Geto-Dacian cultural unity ; and investigations by Soviet archaeologists in the region between the Prut and the Dniester have revealed a Geto-Dacian La Tène culture in this territory also.

GETO-DACIAN CULTURE : GREEK AND ROMAN INFLUENCES

The various contacts between the Geto-Dacians and other peoples which were facilitated by their geographical situation led, as we have seen, to the appearance of coined money. Military, religious and civil architecture had also attained a high level of development. This architecture calls for further study, taking account not only of Greek and Hellenistic influences but also of the Thracian Hallstatt traditions, in which the use of wood, earth and stone was known and practised. Mediterranean influence can be clearly detected in the layout of the buildings and the arrangement of the rooms, particularly in the apsed structures. Another feature which has only recently been observed is the multi-purpose character of certain buildings — shrines and sacred areas, as at Grădiştea Muncelului — previously thought to have had an exclusively religious function. The excavations directed by the present author in fortress No. 1 at Ocniţa (Ocnele Mari) in 1973 revealed the foundations, hewn from the bed-rock, of a building which was both a religious shrine and a palace, a structure of one or two storeys built with oak beams. The material recovered from the underground rooms included fragments of a *dolium* with an inscription in Greek characters. The inscription contains the word *basileus*, though the name of the ruler so designated remains unknown. The same site yielded two sherds bearing the name of a Thracian tribe, the Burii : an important find which made it possible to locate the Bouridauensioi referred to by Ptolemy in the Sub-Carpathians of north-eastern Oltenia and the western part of the district of Argeş. The Dacian town of Buridava must thus have been at Ocniţa (which had rich deposits of salt), and the unnamed *basileus* was the chief of the Burii, exercising military, political and religious authority over this Dacian tribal group. The name " Marco [u] ", no doubt preceded by the word *pronoia* (" by the care of "), may be that of a priest, providing confirmation of the active part played by the priestly class in the life of the Geto-Dacians, comparable with the rôle of the druids in Celtic society. The site is closely dated by two coins of Augustus. The material recovered also included a number of painted vases and a bronze mask *(Plate 48)*, probably representing a male divinity, no doubt the god of war, Mars-Ares. All this goes to indicate the sacred character of the residence of the *basileus*, the military leader of the tribe.

These finds show that the Geto-Dacians used both the Greek and Latin alphabets, and probably that they knew both these languages. This is a fact of considerable historical importance, since it establishes that the Geto-Dacians used the Latin alphabet and knew the Latin language in the time of Augustus, and perhaps earlier if account is taken of the local minting of coins of Republican type : i.e. well before the Roman conquest of Dacia in 106 A.D. The present author agrees with the view of those scholars who believe that the two inscriptions stamped on a vase found at Grădiştea Muncelului — the Dacian town of Sarmizegetusa — are written in Latin, that they have nothing to do with the chronology of the Dacian " kings ", and that they contain the names of Decebal and a priest, probably the chief priest. The adoption of the Latin alphabet makes it clear that the foundations of the later romanisation of Dacia were already laid. It is significant also that at Ocniţa we find Latin being used by classes other than the aristocracy and the priests, to whom it is usually said to have been confined : witness, for example, the word REB, which I would interpret as a personal name spelt in the Latin alphabet *(Plate 80)*.

Similarly if we consider religious beliefs we find that in the 1st century B.C. the Geto-Dacians were accustomed to deposit a coin in the tomb beside the dead man, a practice followed in the Greco-Roman world. In the cremation cemetery at Ocniţa, where more than 205 burials were excavated down to 1973, three coins were found, including a Roman coin of the Republican period, dated to 87 B.C., in tomb No. 89. Thus in the field of religious beliefs — a field of most intimate concern and of great conservatism — the Geto-Dacians were within the sphere of influence of the classical world, and more specifically of the Roman world, long before the Roman occupation at the beginning of the 2nd century A.D.

When the finds of Roman imports are plotted on a map we can appreciate the extent of Roman influence and the degree to which the Geto-Dacians were integrated into the Roman economic system. The native peoples of pre-Roman Dacia were not content with acquiring certain luxury objects (tools, ornaments, glass, bronze vessels, etc.) imported from the Roman world, but began to manufacture locally such typically Roman products as the pottery, both painted and plain, found at Ocniţa. It is thus now necessary to reassess Roman policy towards the Geto-Dacians in the light of recent discoveries, with their evidence that as early as the time of Augustus the region south of the Carpathians had come under the direct influence and perhaps under the control of Rome.

The bronze mask from Ocniţa which has already been mentioned *(Plate 48)*, undoubtedly produced in a local workshop, shows both Roman and Celtic influences. The treatment of the hair, along with other details, reflects the Hellenistic manner which was taken over by the Romans. We have also a considerable number of anthropomorphic terracotta figurines, both male and female ; and a human figurine with a horse's head was discovered at Ocniţa in 1973. The figurines so far recovered have clearly a magical function, related to certain cult practices which had a long life in popular belief. Thraco-Getic art, like the art of the Geto-Dacian phase, shows complete continuity ; and in both we find representations of the human figure, reflecting a constant connection with Mediterranean and Greco-Roman art. Human figures continue to appear on the " Delian " cups, local imitations of the original type. Other examples are provided by the so-called " medallion " from Sarmizegetusa, which has been supposed to represent the goddess Bendis but is in fact merely the reproduction in terracotta of a Republican denarius with indented edges, and a fragment of pottery discovered in Bucharest in 1972, the bust of a woman with strongly marked and expressive features.

Particular significance attaches to the coins produced by the Dacians in the period before the 1st century B.C. and to their imitations of the Roman denarius of the Republican period. As early as the 1st century B.C. the indigenous peoples had assimilated many characteristic features of the Republican coins. The animal and floral themes of the Thraco-Getic phase, however, persisted into the later period, when both Dacians and Daco-Romans made use of them within the new syntheses achieved in these regions.

We can conclude, therefore, that the Geto-Dacians had been caught up in the web of Roman power long before they were actually conquered by Rome. This is the explanation of the thorough romanisation of the Dacians which we shall have occasion to consider in a later chapter. The history of Geto-Dacian culture reflects the operation of a very active factor which, moving from south to north, from Getic to Dacian territory, made its effects felt throughout the intra-Carpathian zone and in north-western Romania, bringing these areas within the sphere of a superior culture. This factor was the influence of Greek civilisation. Within a short time after the foundation of the Greek cities on the western shores of the Black Sea this

Greek influence helped to bring about the transition to the second phase of the Iron Age and promoted an active trade with the local aristocracy, at first on the basis of barter and later using the medium of money. As we have seen, the earliest coins were those struck by Histria, which penetrated into the Getic zone, reaching right up to the foot of the mountains. During the Hellenistic period Greek influence worked like yeast, producing an active effervescence throughout the region occupied by the Geto-Dacians, with particularly far-reaching effects in the Getic area. The alternative posed by Vasile Pârvan and Ion Andrieşescu — Greek influence or Roman influence ? — is not now to be understood as a " choice " to be made by the Geto-Dacian world, a possible hesitation between one direction and another. It does, however, link together two different historical phenomena : Hellenism, in its widest and most enduring sense, provided the basis for a continuing relationship between the Thracian world of the Carpathians and the Mediterranean world, and thus helped to accelerate the process of romanisation. In consequence the Geto-Dacian La Tène culture became involved, like that of the Celts, in the development of European civilisation and was thus able to participate in many ways — particularly through its art, incorporating as it did many Oriental elements — in the syntheses achieved in this region under the late Empire, in which the beginnings of the great migrations and the art of the Germanic peoples were also to play a part.

THE FORMATION OF DACO-ROMANIA

III

The Roman conquests in the Balkans and the Danubian regions led to the establishment of the zone of Roman influence, of *Romanitas*, in eastern Europe : an area first defined by Jireček whose boundaries were more precisely drawn by subsequent research. The culminating point in this process was the integration of Dacia into the *orbis romanus*. The bloody wars between Rome and the various Illyrian and Thracian peoples were followed by a process of romanisation, involving the establishment of urban communities, the adoption of the Latin language and the introduction of a new way of life. As Seneca noted, " Roman energy " was to stamp its imprint deeply on a region where " Hellenic grace " had left only a light impression.

In this chapter we shall not be concerned to trace the various stages of the Roman advance until the final conquest of Dacia, but rather to consider certain features which may explain the lasting nature of Roman influence in the Danubian and Carpathian regions.

THE PROCESS OF ROMANISATION

As we have seen, the Geto-Dacians had created a unitary culture of high standard and distinctive individuality, based on ancient Thracian traditions : a culture which, as Vasile Pârvan noted, formed the basis of Daco-Roman culture, as well as of the later Roman and Romanian cultures which succeeded it. Even before the time of Augustus the Geto-Dacians had come into the Roman sphere of influence in many fields — economic, military, political and cultural. Augustus had realised the great military and political importance of the Danube as the frontier of the Empire, just as Caesar had seen the importance of the Rhine ; but while the Rhine formed a boundary between the Celtic and Germanic worlds the Danube — the sacred river of the Geto-Dacians — flowed through the very heart of the territory occupied by the Geto-Moesians.

The Roman advance to the Danube in 46 A.D., with its consequences in the annexation of the whole area south of the Danube, the Pontic region and the Dobrudja (which now became part of Moesia Inferior), broke up the unity of the extensive territories occupied by the Thracians — a unity which was not incompatible with certain local particularisms in the region between the Carpathians and the Balkans. The establishment of the Roman frontier on the Danube destroyed the harmonious geographical pattern of the Geto-Dacian world, based on the river, the Black Sea and the Carpathian backbone, which had hitherto fostered the ethnic and cultural unity of the Geto-Dacians. The old Thracian substratum, however, was not so easily destroyed, and its influence continued to be felt throughout the whole process of romanisation and subsequently. Everywhere in Roman Dacia, in the extra-Carpathian regions and in the Dobrudja, local traditions remained sturdily alive ; and Daco-Roman civilisation was the product of two factors working together, the influence of Rome on the one hand and the survival of older Geto-Dacian traditions on the other.

The profound transformations — economic, social, political and cultural — brought about by romanisation in the area with which we are concerned must be considered in a historical perspective. The first phase was the long period preceding the conquest of Dacia, when the territory south of the Danube was under Roman influence. Although Rome was destined to leave a durable and glorious imprint on the area north of the Danube, this southern area of Romanitas was established at a much earlier date, the first stages being the assertion of Roman authority over the Thracian and Moeso-Getic peoples. When the Romans reached the Danube in the time of Claudius, bringing into the Empire in one form or another all the territories south of the Danube, the area of Romanitas was extended north of the river, beginning with Oltenia, Muntenia and southern Moldavia. Thus the foundations were laid for the later romanisation of Dacia, a territory already favourably disposed to the new culture and way of life.

54

We have already observed that the Geto-Dacians of the Danubian and Carpathian regions had long been involved in the wide-ranging economic system of Rome. During the 1st century B.C. imports from the Roman world increased, the means of exchange being provided by the Republican denarius and Dacian coins of similar type. The diffusion of the Republican denarius throughout Dacia shows the extent to which the territory north of the Danube was caught up in the expanding Roman economy. As the material recovered at Ocniţa, Grădiştea Muncelului and Cetăţeni-Muscel has demonstrated, the indigenous inhabitants knew the Latin language and alphabet. During the reign of Decebal Roman goods were imported in considerable quantities, Roman influence increased in scale and intensity, and the native peoples assimilated many of the material features of Roman civilisation, imitating them as their tastes, traditions and requirements dictated. Evidence of this process is provided by the painted pottery, for example the ware produced by local potters at Ocniţa during the Augustan period *(Plates 81, 82)*, based both on ancient Thracian traditions and on Roman or Romano-Hellenistic prototypes. Roman influence on Dacian military equipment can also be seen before the conquest of 106 A.D., in such items as the bronze mask from Ocniţa *(Plate 48)*; and Trajan's Column shows Dacian warriors equipped with Roman weapons.

In the always sensitive field of religious beliefs the Dacians had adopted the Greco-Roman practice, common throughout the Mediterranean world, of depositing with the dead a coin intended for the dread ferryman Charon. This practice became frequent among the Daco-Romans, as can be attested from Bratei and other Daco-Roman cemeteries.

It seems possible, therefore, that even before the two Dacian wars of 101-102 and 105-106 Oltenia, Muntenia and southern Moldavia were under Roman control, and that probably as early as the time of Augustus they represented a cover zone for the Empire north of the Danube. The results of recent archaeological work, combined with the fact that the Geto-Dacian fortifications along the southern Sub-Carpathians — Polovragi-Gorj,

Buridava-Vîlcea, Cetăţeni-Muscel, Pietroasele (Gruiu)-Buzău, etc. — were destroyed and not subsequently rebuilt, show that the Getic tribes of the extra-Carpathian zone on both sides of the Danube had entered the Roman economic and political sphere and passed under the military control of Rome a century before the time of Decebal. The Dobrudja, which was under direct Roman rule, was a strategic area essential for maintaining Roman authority in the lower Danube region and on the west and north coasts of the Black Sea : from the earliest decades of Roman occupation, therefore, it was exposed to intense romanisation. Faced with the resistance of the native population and with the raids by the Bastarnae and the Sarmatians of which Ovid wrote in his exile at Tomis, the early Emperors concentrated their attention on the lower Danube, preparing the way for the conquest of the Dacian bastion. Numbers of camps and forts were built along the river, and thousands of tribesmen — men, women and children, with their kings and chieftains — were transferred from their homes beyond the Danube to the territory south of the river, which never formed a frontier either in Roman times or during the period of the great migrations.

This situation inclines the present author to agree with Daicoviciu's view that the Roman province of Dacia included the territory which was still under the authority of Decebal when it was invaded in 106.

Romanisation was a complex process, both in terms of time and of depth. The process was not a purely linguistic one — the adoption of spoken Latin by the Thraco-Moeso-Getic and Dacian population — but extended to every aspect of material and spiritual life. Archaeologists have recovered evidence of the changes which took place before the conquest in both material life and spiritual culture. The process of romanisation was promoted in many different ways. The vigour and rapidity with which the process got under way was of course largely due to the large-scale settlement of the province of Dacia which was initiated by Rome. The same policy had been followed in the Dobrudja and — on a lesser scale and by other means — in southern Moldavia and on the left bank of the Danube in

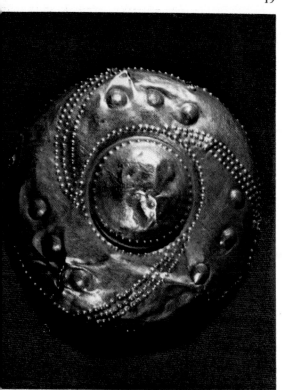

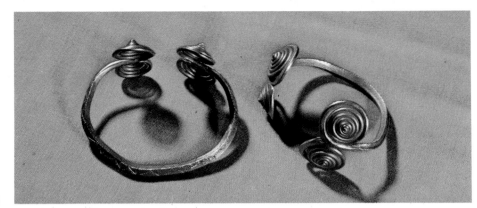

26

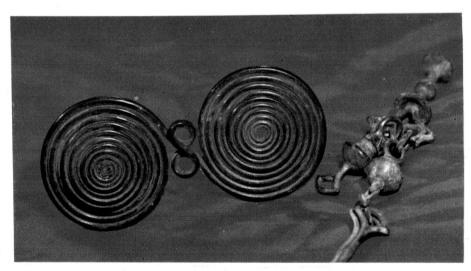

27

28

29

30

31

32

33

34

35

36

37

38

39

40

41

42

43

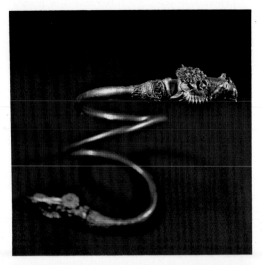

44

45

47   46

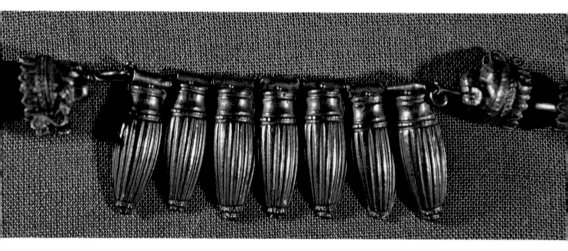

48

50 49

52

51

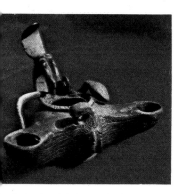

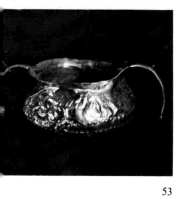

53

54

56

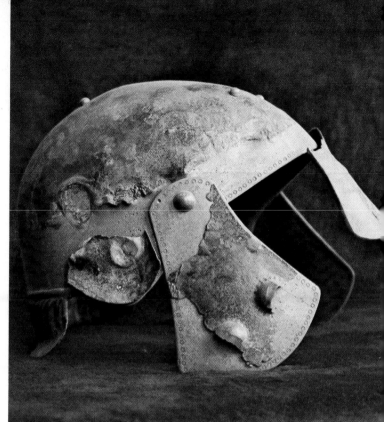

55

57

58

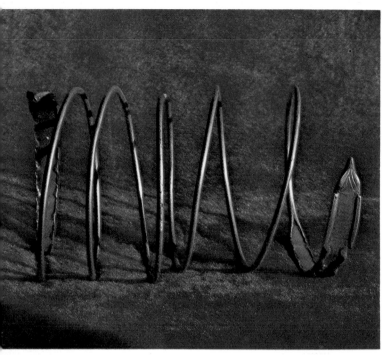

59

60

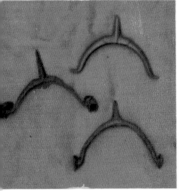

61

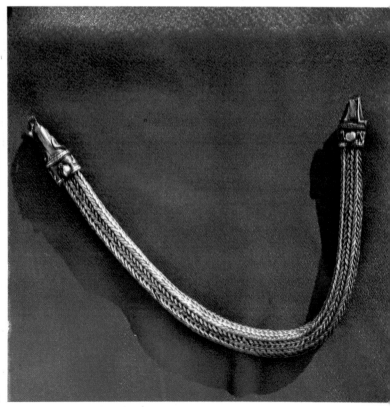

62

Muntenia.   The foundation of towns, either *coloniae* or *municipia*, in the area between the Danube and the Black Sea and in Dacia was one of the principal agencies of romanisation.   The use of the Latin language was promoted by the involvement of the native population in the Roman economic system and the recruitment of Dacians into the Roman army ; and the constitution promulgated by Caracalla in the year 212 granted the free population of Dacia, as of the rest of the Empire, the privileges of Roman citizenship.

The army played a particularly significant rôle in the romanisation of Dacia, which was an Imperial province.   Round the military camps there grew up civilian settlements *(canabae)* occupied by the soldiers and their families, and some of these settlements were given the status of towns.   On completing their long term of service in the army (anything up to 25 years) veterans were given a grant of land and Roman citizenship for themselves and their wives and children, and most of them settled in the country, becoming members of a rural community in which they enjoyed respect and prestige.   The Romanian word *bătrin* ("old") is derived from *veteranus* (found in the form *beteranus* in inscriptions of the late period), and the tradition of these retired warriors, with a reputation for achievement and experience, survived in Romania throughout the Middle Ages.

The exceptionally high number (some 3000) of inscriptions written in Latin provides evidence that in some cases the romanisation of a Dacian family was achieved within the space of three generations : the name of the last descendant gives no hint that he had a Thraco-Getic grandfather.

Romanisation did not, of course, proceed at the same pace over the whole of Geto-Dacian territory, but showed variations from area to area.   In Scythia Minor, on both banks of the Danube and in Roman Dacia the population was thoroughly romanised, but the process went more slowly in rural areas, even in territory under direct Roman rule : in such areas there was no doubt a period of bilingualism.   By the same token, the Geto-Dacian La Tène culture at first continued to develop in parallel with the formation of a Roman provincial civilisation (i.e. the official urban culture as distinct from the Daco-Roman or Geto-Moeso-Dacian culture).

Thus as a result of the fact that it was romanised at a time when the Roman world as a whole was in process of expansion " Dacia preserved its Roman heritage intact, and the Romance basis of its language withstood Slav and Turkish influence " (G.A. Mansuelli, *The Cultures of Ancient Europe*, 1967, p. 326).

THE RÔLE OF THE FREE DACIANS

The part played by the free Dacians in maintaining the continuity of romanisation and the ethnic and cultural unity of the Daco-Romans has become apparent only in the light of the most recent archaeological work ; nor has sufficient attention been paid in the past to the influence of the geographical setting — varying according to differing local circumstances — in preserving the ethnic and linguistic unity of the Romanian people in the early stages of its formation.   A glance at Map A shows that the Roman province of Dacia was surrounded on three sides by free Dacians who had direct links with the Romans.   The large numbers of Roman coins found in Muntenia and Moldavia and in the Crişana and Maramureş districts, together with the imports from the Roman world, the imitations of Roman products and the assimilation of certain Roman technological skills (e.g. in the making of pottery), show that the free Dacians living beyond the frontiers of the Empire had been drawn into the economic and political orbit of Rome.   Along the frontiers of Dacia and on the lower Danube they remained in regular contact with their fellow-countrymen within the province who were continually exposed to the process of romanisation. They thus represented a living reservoir of national feeling available to promote the resurgence of the Dacian element in Daco-Roman civilisation.

Thus through the involvement of the free Dacians in the process of romanisation and in the formation of Daco-Roman civilisation the ethnic and cultural unity of earlier times was re-established, but now in a Daco-Roman form. In the new circumstances created by the Roman withdrawal from Dacia in 271 the historical rôle of the native Dacian peoples, who had in large part maintained their traditions and organisation within their own communities beyond the frontiers of Roman rule, took on exceptional significance. It is now well established that it was not the Goths who moved into the Roman province after 271, but the free Dacians. The excavations carried out by G. Bichir in 1973 at Stolniceni (district of Vîlcea) on the Roman site of Buridava revealed that the remains of the Roman camp were overlaid by a cultural level belonging to the Dacians and not to the Goths. The Goths themselves did not enter the former Roman province of Dacia until the beginning of the 4th century, when they came not to settle but to establish military camps. The activities of the free Dacians — the Daci Magni, the Costoboci and the Carpi — are recorded by a number of writers and attested by inscriptions. A number of Roman Emperors, both before and after Aurelian, assumed the style of Carpicus or Dacicus after their expeditions against these doughty warriors who still maintained the traditions of Burebista and Decebal. The remains excavated at Poieneşti in Moldavia are to be attributed to the Carpi, on the evidence of the funerary ritual, based on cremation and the preservation of the ashes in lidded urns (some of them of a type harking back to ancient Dacian traditions), and other features characteristic of the Geto-Dacian La Tène culture. In addition to the strong Roman influence we have already noted the culture of the Carpi shows certain features of Sarmatian origin, like a very distinctive type of mirror and vases with zoomorphic handles.

The free Dacians had an influence on the Puchow and Lipitsa cultures, and in the present writer's view it was through their agency that certain features of Roman civilisation were transmitted to the ancient Slavs, as is shown by a number of words of Latin origin which the Slavs took over at an early period, before their expansion into the Balkans and Central Europe. The preservation in Romanian of certain Thraco-Geto-Dacian words can be more readily explained through the agency of the free Dacians than that of the conquered population, subject as they were to more than a century and a half of Roman rule.

Thus the geographical basis of romanisation is seen to be much wider than the Roman province of Dacia. The process of formation of the Romanian people and their language took place over a very extensive area, reaching beyond the territory of Daco-Romania in the Carpatho-Danubian region into the areas where the free Dacians adapted the Roman way of life to the conditions of their rural communities, and taking in the territories south of Danube as far as the " Jireček line ". Outside this area there were other Latinised zones in the Balkans. It is worth noting also that these romanised regions south of the Danube, living an urban life within the Roman and later the Byzantine Empire, remained in close contact with the romanised population of Dacia even during the migration period.

Linguistically, as A. Rosetti noted, the eastern area of Romanitas — and thus also the Carpatho-Danubio-Pontic region — is distinct from the western language group ; and its material and spiritual culture is likewise distinct from that of the West. The Thracian and Geto-Dacian substratum in this area, whose enduring vitality is still a unifying factor in South-East Europe, left its distinctive imprint on every manifestation of the life and culture of this eastern Romanitas.

THE DACIAN ELEMENT IN ROMAN DACIA

The Dacians were by no means wiped out in their wars with the Romans, and there is much evidence of their continuing existence in Roman Dacia. More than fifteen military units, like the Cohors I Aelia Dacorum, were recruited from the Dacian population and sent to various parts of the Empire. Later, in the 3rd century, native troops were enrolled to meet local needs, supplementing the regular Roman forces stationed in the province. Another proof of the continuity of the same population in the land of their ancestors is provided by the names of rivers and towns in Dacia, most of which were preserved during the Roman period.

In the field of material culture the Geto-Dacians took over new forms and techniques from the Romans, but also preserved a whole series of traditional elements. Among these was the typical Dacian cup, serving a variety of purposes, which is still found in rural settlements of the Roman period like Cristeşti and Lechinţa de Mureş and in cemeteries, as well as in Roman military camps like Micia, Mehadia, Orheiul Bistriţei, Breţcu and Rîşnov. At Rîşnov large quantities of locally made pottery were discovered, suggesting that the troops occupying this camp were recruited from the native population ; and this was also the case at other camps, at any rate to some extent. Another type of vessel used for the storage of provisions, the *dolium*, which was in common use in the Dacian cities, also continued in favour after the Roman withdrawal and is still found in the 4th century, with the same shape and the same type of decoration (a band of wavy lines). Although romanised, the Dacians maintained their traditional funerary practice of cremation, evidence of which has been found at Soporu de Cîmpie, Ighiu, Caşolţ, Sighişoara and other sites.

ROMAN PROVINCIAL ART IN DACIA

The art of Roman Dacia, like that of other provinces, reflected the stage in the evolution of Roman art reached at the time of the Roman conquest. The older substratum out of which this art grew, however, gave it distinctive characteristics which became more marked under the late Empire. In addition to works reflecting the style of the period, with its particular political, social and religious elements, we find a whole series of more modest works of art produced for the poorer classes of the population (veterans, craftsmen, peasants, freed slaves, etc.) which show local features, to some extent representing a revival of very ancient traditions. This popular art runs counter to the ideals of classical Greco-Roman art and is notable for its primitive character, its naivety and its naturalism. This phenomenon is not peculiar to Dacia, but is found in the other peripheral provinces of the Roman world. In this respect, however, Dacia was in a special position, since it had produced before the Roman conquest a local art in which the ancient Thracian tradition had been enriched by creative impulses from Greece, the Hellenistico-Roman world and Rome. Moreover the Roman provincial art of Dacia and the lower Danube region developed within a population which was not only considerable in numerical terms but enjoyed a high level of civilisation. And finally the free Dacians living beyond the Roman frontiers exerted some influence on Roman art within the province, the Sarmatians contributed some features characteristic of " barbarian " art, and other Oriental characteristics were brought in by settlers from the eastern provinces of the Empire.

The Geto-Dacians living in the territories conquered by Rome contributed to the development and transformation of Roman provincial art. We find in the Roman art of Dacia and the lower Danube region motifs stemming from ancient Thraco-Getic traditions, like the heroised Thracian horseman and the Danubian horseman. Some of the carving on the trophy monument at Adamclisi was the work of romanised native sculptors, making this a document of inestimable value for the history of Romania, comparable in this respect with Trajan's Column. The Adamclisi carvings show great expressive power, a resurgence of very ancient geometric motifs and a primitive realism of markedly popular character. Thus although the Roman provincial art of Dacia shows many features of western origin its specific local characteristics give it a very distinctive aspect of its own.

THE PERIOD OF
THE FIRST MIGRATIONS

IV

In the reign of Aurelian (271-275), following the incursions of the Carpi and the Goths into Moesia and other provinces in the Balkans, a new situation was created in the lower Danube region.   Roman Dacia, Rome's last conquest, was officially evacuated, and thus became the first province to be abandoned in the Empire's time of social and economic crisis.   The statements of the Pseudo-Vopiscus *(sublato exercitu et provincialibus)* and Eutropius *(abductos Romanos ex urbibus et agris Daciae)* have led some historians to talk of a total evacuation of the population of Dacia and of its occupation by the Goths (" Gothia ") and subsequently by the Slavs (" Sclavinia ").   With the help of archaeology, however, it is possible to come nearer to the truth of the matter.

THE ROMAN AND ROMANO-BYZANTINE PRESENCE NORTH OF THE DANUBE

The abandonment of Dacia was a military and administrative operation : it did not involve a transfer of population — a process which would have been impossible of achievement at that period — nor did it represent a withdrawal from the province in favour of the Romans' Gothic *foederati*.   The Goths did not in any event enter Dacia until later : in this region they were anticipated by the Dacian Carpi, whose military power was destroyed by Diocletian and Maximian, who then resettled part of the tribe south of the Danube in Moesia.   The Romans continued to patrol the Danube, and a considerable area north of the river remained in Roman hands : the Danube was still a Roman river.   Throughout the length of the Roman occupied zone a series of fortresses and of towns like Drobeta, Sucidava and Constantiniana Daphne remained as centres of Roman civilisation and as markets for the native population.   On several occasions Roman Emperors took military action against their Gothic or Sarmatian allies, either by mounting expeditions, as Constantine did, or by erecting fortifications, like Justinian ; and Constantine also built a stone bridge over the Danube at Sucidava.   As a result of this policy Rome still held out possibilities of development to the indigenous peoples, even in this time of troubles, and the process of romanisation continued.

Thus it can be seen that the so-called " abandonment " of Dacia did not amount to a complete break with the past and that the former province was not transformed into a desert overnight. The existence in the 4th and 5th centuries of a region south of the Danube where Roman civilisation was firmly established and continued to flourish, in spite of attacks by the nomadic peoples (mainly Goths and Huns), served as a reserve and a reinforcement for the romanised and Latin-speaking peoples north of the Danube. This process of fertilisation operated in different ways — through voluntary movements into a region where the Roman way of life persisted only in rural and popular forms but where it was possible to escape from the exactions of Roman or Romano-Byzantine tax-collectors, or as a result of expeditions by the Romans or the nomadic peoples across the Danube. The river was not by any means an uncrossable frontier ; moreover it would not have been possible for shipping to move freely to and fro if the Romans had not held the left bank.

It is clear, therefore, that the Romans did not entirely abandon the territory of Dacia. The evidence of archaeology, coins and the written sources attests that they held on to a zone on the north bank of the Danube from the end of the 3rd to the beginning of the 6th century. The archaeological material recovered from a series of Roman camps and towns reflects the continuance of civil and military life. Material dating from the time of Constantine, who extended the zone north of the Danube, proves the presence of the Romans at Drobeta, the camp of Putineiu and elsewhere. Recent discoveries at Drobeta, made during the 1970 excavations, point to the urban character of the site and have revealed the presence of workshops near the walls of the camp, which were strengthened in the 4th century. A similar situation is found at the *castrum* of Pietroasele (district of Buzău), excavated in 1973. In both cases Roman and Daco-Roman remains predominate in the archaeological material recovered. In the time of Constantine an earth *vallum* was constructed from west to east, linking the *castra* of Drobeta, Putineiu and Pietroasele, fortified outposts in a territory which was not ill disposed to Roman authority. Archaeological work in the Iron Gates area has given concrete proof of the measures taken by the Romans to ensure the safe passage of shipping in the Cazane-Clisura stretch of the river (the Pojogina camp, the *castella* of Gornea and Sviniţa, and the *castrum* of Drobeta, to say nothing of other strong points on the lower Danube). We see the Romans' firm intention from the outset to regard Dacia as Imperial territory.

The world of eastern Romanitas consolidated its position in the period following the reign of Aurelian. From this region came the main military forces for the defence of the frontier ; and here too were born a number of Emperors and illustrious generals like Aetius, the conqueror of Attila. Thanks to the particular economic and social situation, the important part played in these territories by the romanised peasants, the firmly established pattern of urban life and the reforms carried out during the late Empire from the time of Diocletian onwards, the eastern Empire met the barbarian threat with a well conceived policy centred on the Danube region. At the time of the first migrations the existence on both sides of the Danube of a vigorous romanised culture in its Greco-Roman form (attested by the example of Scythia Minor : see the volume on " Romania " in this series) extending round the Black Sea coast to the Crimea provides an explanation for the fact that Daco-Romania did not become part of the barbarian world (" Barbaricum ") but maintained its Dacian and Roman traditions, which achieved a new synthesis during the 4th and 5th centuries, in the time of the Huns. This Danubio-Pontic Romanitas, like the rest of the eastern territories of the Empire, exerted considerable influence on the barbarian peoples, in particular the Germanic peoples, who assimilated the Roman way of life, taking over numerous elements of Roman material and spiritual culture and adapting them to their social and economic needs and to their La Tène traditions.

The art of the Germanic peoples, a decorative art of little figurative interest, depended on techniques — cloisonné and champlevé, filigree, granulation, etc. — which came into use during the late Empire. Although the first shock of the barbarian invasions led to much devastation, destruction and pillage they did not result in the displacement of the settled population from the lands to which they were so firmly attached. Roman civilisation — an all-embracing European urban civilisation — represented a unifying factor : in the words of René Grousset (1946), " We find Roman influence, acting through a variety of intermediaries, at the basis of every nation ". In spite of the germanisation of the western Roman world, the partial slavonicisation of the eastern Roman world and the asianisation of the Greek world, there was a resurgence of the Roman spirit throughout Europe in the 9th, 10th and 11th centuries, when the various European peoples, including the Romance peoples, emerged as distinct ethnic entities. Among these new peoples was the Romanian people.

Seen in this light, the ethnogenesis of the Romanian people is no longer an enigma ; nor is it a miracle, unless the appearance of a particular people or individual in a given geographical setting and at a given period of history is always to be regarded as a miracle. But, miracle or not, it is the task of the historian to trace its development and identify the historical realities of that development.

THE MASTERS OF THE LAND

V

Throughout this time of troubles, relieved by occasional short periods of stability and of cultural synthesis, assimilation or overlay, there remained one immovable foundation — the indigenous population with its capacity for endurance, mobility, polarisation and development. During the tormented period of the migrations the native peoples, first Daco-Roman and later fully romanised, were, in Nicolae Iorga's apt phrase, the " masters of the land ". During the last thirty years Romanian archaeologists have recovered the material remains of these masters of the land — sometimes reflecting a culture of primitive character, sometimes comprising objects of more elaborate workmanship, usually found scattered over a wide area but in some cases concentrated on sites of more limited extent, and always based on the same ancient Geto-Dacian and Roman traditions. Associated with these remains are Roman and later Romano-Byzantine and Byzantine imports, together with coins of the same periods — all combining to demonstrate that the Carpatho-Danubio-Pontic region remained constantly within the ambit of the eastern Roman world.

The archaeological material of the period after 300 A.D. — which can be taken as the beginning of the migration period proper — falls into two main groups. The first group is attributable to the indigenous peoples, attached from time immemorial to the same land and mainly occupied in agriculture and stock-rearing ; the second belongs to the migrant peoples with their own distinctive cultures. Each of these migrant groups, and particularly those which came into closest contact with the native peoples, left their mark on the culture of the region, making a contribution which Romanian historians agree in regarding as beneficial ; and this contribution was handed on to the Romanian people. As Iorga wrote in 1936, Romanian history " has undoubtedly been influenced by all those nations that have passed over an area extending considerably beyond that of Dacia itself, which constituted now a place of refuge and now a point of departure, and particularly by the nations which stayed longest within this geographical area and thereby contributed to the formation of the Romanian people ".

83

There is no suggestion, during the period after 300 A.D., of any abandonment of agriculture by the native peoples, of their withdrawal to the mountains or of their reversion to a pastoral economy. Archaeological discoveries in the plain country have demonstrated the contrary. Distinguished philologists like Rosetti have shown by the study of agricultural terminology that agriculture continued to be practised alongside stock-rearing. The continuing presence of Romanians even in the plain areas is also attested by certain place names in the heart of the Romanian plain, like Vlăsia and Codrul Vlăsiei or Vlaşca, from the Slav term *Vlahi*, applied to peoples speaking a Romance tongue.

In seeking to understand the ethnic and linguistic structures of Romanian culture it must always be borne in mind that what gave the Romanian language its distinctive character was the Thracian and Moeso-Geto-Dacian substratum, which represented a factor of linguistic continuity. In the field of Daco-Roman material culture it was the Geto-Dacian element combined with the Roman contribution that maintained the unbroken continuity which we have already noted. The early Slavs likewise left their mark on the culture and language of the native peoples, giving them an imprint quite distinct from those of the other Romance peoples of western Europe. In parallel with the formation, between the 2nd and 4th centuries, of the language known to linguists as Eastern Latin (a popular Latin spoken in Moesia, Dacia and the neighbouring regions) there evolved a simplified Daco-Roman civilisation which the " masters of the land " made into a demographic and ethnic force of decisive significance. The grafting of Roman civilisation on to a pre-Roman substratum gave rise to a unitary Daco-Roman culture and a unified Romance language, without dialectal variation, throughout the Carpatho-Danubio-Pontic region. In the view of most Romanian philologists Slav influence on the language of the native Romance-speakers began to make itself felt not at the end of the 6th century, when the presence of the Slavs in Daco-Romania is attested by archaeological evidence, but much later. The Slavs did not in fact change the basic Romance structure (the essential vocabulary, the morphology, the phonology) of the Romanian language, though in the field of material culture, as revealed by archaeology (see Chapter VIII), their influence is more evident. At any rate it is possible by the 7th century to talk of a Proto-Romanian people.

DACO-ROMAN CONTINUITY

During the early migration period Daco-Romania was no more than an area of passage for those migrant peoples of Iranian, Germanic or Asiatic origin who settled only sporadically in the territory occupied by the Daco-Romans, the main centre of their power lying to the east (in the case of the Goths) or to the west (in the case of the Huns, the Gepidae and the Avars). Certain other peoples who entered Daco-Romania, like the Sarmatians — the Iazyges, the Roxolani and the Alans — were assimilated soon after the Hunnic invasion in 376. One consequence of this invasion was a move south of the Danube by the Visigoths in 376, leaving the Ostrogoths under the domination of the Huns who had established themselves in the puszta. The archaeological evidence demonstrates the continued presence of the indigenous peoples — Romans, romanised Dacians and free Dacians — in the region lying beyond the frontiers of the Roman Empire. This continuity of life and culture is found not only among the peoples of Trajan's former province (Transylvania and particularly Oltenia, an area of intense romanisation) but throughout the whole of Daco-Romania. During this period, as we have already seen, the free Dacians (amongst whom the Carpo-Dacians still constituted a danger to the Empire) were involved in a process of Roman cultural and linguistic acculturation ; and in association with the Romans and the romanised population of the former province they laid the foundations of a synthesis which in the time of the Goths reached its full flowering in the Sîntana de Mureş-Chernyakhov culture. Concrete evidence of this process has been provided by the excavations carried out within the last thirty years in accordance with the desiderata set out before the second world war by Ion Andrieşescu, one of the founders of Romanian prehistoric and protohistorical archaeology.

The archaeology of the lst millennium and the mediaeval period, as recently developed in Romania, is of a different character from prehistoric archaeology. It cannot confine itself to enumerating the physical remains in order to determine the stage of development reached by a particular population or society, since it possesses historical sources and linguistic evidence which make possible an objective and scientific historical interpretation of the material from the ethnic point of view. It is this type of approach that reveals the continuous presence throughout Daco-Romania in the early migration period (4th-6th centuries) of peasant communities and villages : i.e. of a rural population of stock-herders and farmers not belonging to the migrant peoples but remaining within the Daco-Roman tradition.

Apart from the remains found north of the Danube in the territory under direct Roman control, it is notable that some ruined Roman towns and urban centres were still inhabited by Romans and romanised Dacians. This has been established, for example, at Apulum (Alba Iulia), where excavation yielded knobbed bronze fibulas dating from the 4th century and a cemetery of tombs built of kiln-fired bricks between the ruined walls of public buildings. In addition to the fibulas the burials contained bracelets of Roman type and beads and coins of the Constantinian period. On the site of the town of Napoca (Cluj) and in the surrounding area the excavators recovered numbers of coins, silver fibulas of Pontic origin with semi-discs, bronze and silver pendants with cube-shaped terminals, fibulas with a semicircular head ending in three knobs, of a type derived from Ponto-Gothic models, etc. During the 4th century, when the towns of Daco-Romania were flickering into extinction, the sparse population which still inhabited the ruins no doubt adopted a rural way of life, which was to become general in the 5th century. Evidence of this phase is provided by the Romanian words *pămint* (land) and *sat* (village), derived respectively

86

from *pavimentum* (pavement, floor) and *fossatum* (defensive ditch). The word *sat* points to the existence of a stable population concerned with the fortification and defence of their settlements, threatened by the movement of the migrant peoples.

During this period the free Dacians living in the north and west of the former Dacia Traiana and the Carpo-Dacians represented a significant military and political force until their defeat by Diocletian and Maximian. Thereafter some of the Carpi were forcibly resettled south of the Danube, but most of the free Dacians remained in Daco-Romania, as is shown by much archaeological evidence, and contributed to the formation of a cultural synthesis which found expression in the Bratei culture. The presence of the free Dacians is attested, for example, by hand-made and wheel-turned pottery of Dacian workmanship and by cremation cemeteries (like the one at Cipău in Transylvania) indicating penetration by Dacians from the west. The archaeological material, including both items of Roman workmanship and objects produced by Dacians in imitation of Roman prototypes, show the appeal which Roman civilisation had long held for the free Dacians of the west (the Crişana and Maramureş regions). The departure of the Roman authorities created the conditions necessary for the formation of a unitary culture, which came about after the assimilation of other elements contributed by the earliest migrant peoples, the Sarmatians and Goths.

THE SARMATIANS AND GOTHS IN DACO-ROMANIA

The Sarmatians, a nomadic Iranian people of stock-herders and warlike horsemen, had been in contact with the Geto-Dacians before the beginning of the Christian era and had exerted some influence on them, detectable during the Roman period in the Poieneşti-Chilia culture. There were some Sarmatian infiltrations into the territories inhabited by the Geto-Dacians, but although the Iazyges settled in western Dacia about the middle of the lst century A.D. the other Sarmatians (the Roxolani and the Alans) — who were in any event fewer in numbers — did not make any large-scale penetration until the 3rd century, under pressure from the Goths. The redoubtable mail-clad horsemen, the *cataphractarii*, were then more lightly armed, and were perhaps under the control of the Goths. Their presence on Romanian territory is attested by the existence of cremation cemeteries, with grave goods which include mirrors with monograms in relief *(tamgas)* on the back which no doubt had a magical and apotropaic significance, swords with hilts ending in a ring, fibulas, etc. Women's tombs contain beads made of glass, amber, coral and semi-precious stones, which were either made up into necklaces or sewn into the hem of garments. The practice of cranial deformation, a custom of Asiatic origin also found among the Huns, is attested among the Sarmatians, particularly the Alans. As for the Sarmatian Iazyges, recent excavations have shown that they occupied only the plain region in the west of the Banat. The lower Mureş basin has produced evidence of considerable Dacian settlement : witness, for example, the Dacian towns of Pecica and Soimuş, on the banks of the Mureş. Roman occupation is also confirmed by archaeological evidence extending as far as the confluence of the Mureş and the Tisza.

In the 4th century A.D. there were numerous indigenous settlements which still maintained regular contact with the Roman world south of the Danube. The written sources also mention the Sarmatians, always with reference to the Iazyges. Ammianus Marcellinus records that in 332 they asked the Emperor Constantine for help against the Goths and that the Emperor came to their assistance and inflicted a great defeat on the Goths. Later, however, a conflict broke out within the Sarmatian confederation, between the Argaragantes and the Limigantes. The Limigantes, who according to Ammianus Marcellinus were the slaves of the Argaragantes, defeated their masters with the help of the weapons supplied for use against the Goths. Some authors assert that the Limigantes were Daco-Romans who had become subject to the Iazyges. Whether this is

63

64

65

66

67

68

70

71

69

72

73

74

75

76

77

78

79

80

81

82

83

84

85

86

87

89

88

93   92

true or not, the Sarmatians disappeared soon after the tumult caused by the Hunnic invasions, at the end of the 4th century, having made their contribution to the new culture which is associated with the name of the Goths.

Sweeping down in successive waves from their territory of " Gothia " and the shores of the Baltic towards the Black Sea, the Goths established themselves in the wooded steppe land, and during the 3rd century, with the Carpi as their allies, launched a series of raids against the Roman Empire, ravaging the towns of Tanais, Olbia and Tyras. As a result of this contact with the Greco-Roman world of the Pontic region the social cleavage within Gothic society became more marked, and the Goths took over many features of Pontic civilisation, an amalgam of many diverse factors which rose to great importance in the later Empire and the early migration period. The art of the Goths, like that of all the migrant peoples, was a princely art. Unlike the nomadic peoples of the steppes, however, they practised agriculture. Accordingly they created a culture of heterogeneous character, both within their original area of settlement and in the territories into which they expanded. Studies carried out since the second world war into the Sîntana de Mureş culture on the territory of Romania have led to conclusions of great interest, detailed analysis of the material recovered in the excavations of the last 25 or 30 years having shown that this culture must be attributed to peoples of Germanic origin, and specifically to the Goths.

In this heterogeneous culture Germanic elements are predominant. The theory formerly in favour which regarded the Chernyakhov culture (known in Romania as the Sîntana de Mureş culture, from the site of that name in the district of Mureş in Transylvania) as being of Slav origin is now shown to be erroneous. Excavations were carried out at Sîntana de Mureş by I. Kovács at the beginning of this century, the results being published at Cluj in 1912. Immediately after the first world war Ion Andrieşescu began to excavate the Oinac-Giurgiu cemetery — the first excavations of the kind in the extra-Carpathian region of Romania. During the second world war, and more particularly after 1944, systematic excavation was carried out at various places in Romania, leading to the publication of a number of detailed studies and important monographs which are listed in the Bibliography. It is now well established that this culture was widely diffused, extending in the west as far as the barrier of the mountains. Oltenia has yielded relatively little material of Sîntana de Mureş type, but in the rest of Romania abundant evidence of this culture has been recovered : in addition to Sîntana de Mureş itself and the site at Oinac, Sîntana de Mureş material has been found in the cemeteries of Spanţov, Tîrgşor, Olteni, Gherăseni, Independenţa, Mogoşani, Erbiceni-Iaşi, Ciumbrud, Sf. Gheorghe, etc.

The Sîntana de Mureş culture was formed in the upper and middle valley of the Dnieper, from which the migrations to the west and south-west were launched. A number of different strains can be identified as contributing to its formation and structure. It shows certain Roman features resulting from contacts between the Germanic world and the higher civilisation of the Romans : evidence of this is provided, for example, by the famous treasure of Pietroasele, belonging to the Ostrogoths and probably dating from the early 5th century, some items in which show the influence of Roman prototypes and techniques used in Roman workshops *(Plates 114-117)*. There is also a Sarmatian element, with features characteristic of the Iranian steppe peoples, which reflects the close relationships between the Sarmatians and the Goths. This Sarmatian element is much more evident in the eastern sector of the Sîntana de Mureş complex than in the central and western sectors, where the Dacian element is more marked.

The picture emerging from recent archaeological work in Romania is quite clear. Although the predominant element in the Chernyakhov-Sîntana de Mureş culture was supplied by the Goths, it is firmly established that the indigenous peoples played a significant part in the genesis of that culture. It was this romanised indigenous world, with all its internal differentiation, that formed an element of continuity and encouraged the settlement of the migrant Germanic peoples in Geto-Dacian territory, then in process of becoming Romance. It can readily be shown that in Muntenia, for example — where an abundance of 4th century archaeological material has been recovered — the Latin language was known, written and of course spoken. Thus we have a sherd of Curcani-Ilfov pottery with the name Mitis incised on it and a fragment of a dish, of crude workmanship but nevertheless bearing the maker's proud inscription *Aurelius Silvanus fecit pataelam bonam.* This latter piece, from Socetu (district of Teleorman), is now in the museum at Roşiori de Vede. Ulfila, who translated the Bible into Gothic in the 4th century and preached in that language to the Gothic population of what is now Muntenia, also preached in Latin to the indigenous peoples of Romance tongue. Similarly the presence of St Sabas in north-eastern Muntenia in 372 and the fact that he was drowned in the river Buzău for preaching Christianity indicate that the population of this region included not only Goths but indigenous Romance-speakers. Excavations by G. Diaconu in the Pietroasele camp in 1973 produced evidence of occupation by both Goths and indigenous inhabitants, and Mişu Davidescu has recently recovered similar evidence from the 4th-5th century fortress at Drobeta.

It is clear, therefore, that in historical and archaeological terms the Sîntana de Mureş culture can be understood only if account is taken of the indigenous elements in its composition and of the relationships between the Goths and the Roman Empire.

At this point it is appropriate to recall the evidence produced by recent archaeological work that when the Roman troops and administration withdrew from Dacia it was not the Goths who invaded the province, as was formerly thought, but the indigenous population from the neighbouring regions : i.e. the free Dacians, themselves already involved in the process of romanisation. The stratigraphic investigation carried out in 1973 by G.

Bichir in the Roman fortress of Buridava at Stolniceni on the Olt showed that the level overlying the Roman level gave evidence not of Gothic culture but of the culture of the free population living east of the Olt. An indigenous settlement at Hărman-Braşov in south-eastern Transylvania, the development of which continued throughout the 4th century, yielded early elements of the Sîntana de Mureş culture, which continued to develop east of the Carpathians. By detailed examination of certain features of Gothic culture Kurt Horedt was able to establish that the Goths did not enter Transylvania until about the second half of the 4th century, and that they evacuated it in the first half of the 5th, under pressure from the Huns : the first to enter the region were always the free Dacians from the west and north-west. Material recently found in the Crişana and Maramureş districts (Map A) shows many affinities with material from the former province. Similarly the occurrence of Roman coins and other Roman features demonstrates — as it does also for Moldavia, Bucovina and Muntenia — that the unity of the Geto-Dacian element in the population was maintained even during the Roman occupation. It was in this area that Daco-Roman unity (so clearly reflected in the archaeological material recovered during the last thirty years) was firmly established, so that neither the Sarmatians nor the Goths were able to destroy it. It continued to consolidate itself after the year 271 and for a further century, freely and without interference from the migrant peoples. In Horedt's view there is no room for doubt about Daco-Roman continuity in Transylvania during the century between the Roman withdrawal from Dacia and the Gothic invasion ; and this view is supported by precise archaeological evidence and a coherent historical interpretation, with which the present author entirely agrees.

THE HUNS IN DACO-ROMANIA

In 376 the Huns, who in the previous year had reached the Don and were now continuing their westward advance, won a victory over the Goths. One branch of the Goths, the Visigoths, sought the protection of the Romano-Byzantine Empire and moved south of the Danube, while the Ostrogoths submitted to their conquerors. The Sîntana de Mureş culture continued to develop throughout the last quarter of the 4th century and beyond, but then gradually died out as its traditions were imperceptibly assimilated by the " masters of the land ". In the conditions of insecurity and instability prevailing in the late 4th and the 5th centuries the only force capable of maintaining historical and ethnic continuity in the Carpathians and the Danube region was the indigenous Romance-speaking population. The existence of this population as providers of a food supply was absolutely necessary to the new masters of the territory, the Huns who had now supplanted the previous Germanic rulers. The destruction of Germanic power did not, as might have been supposed, lead to disastrous consequences for the conquered population. Archaeological evidence proves the continuance during the Hunnic occupation of scattered groups of Goths, who were gradually absorbed by the native population or else moved on towards the west or south.

The Huns, a people of nomadic warriors, imposed their authority not only by force of arms but also in virtue of their better organisation and their flexible policy towards the conquered peoples. They settled in the plain of the Tisza and the middle Danube, but launched raids aimed at pillage and intimidation throughout the Carpatho-Danubian region. Attila's expeditions of 442 and 447 finally extinguished the last remnants of urban life in the regions of Roman culture north of the Danube and in the Carpathians. The towns and fortifications built or rebuilt by Constantine were destroyed : the written sources speak of seventy towns, including Sucidava, pillaged and destroyed by Attila. Throughout Daco-Romania the indigenous population adopted a rural way of life centred on villages. Some scholars, indeed, were inclined until recently to believe that in the 5th and later centuries the native peoples ceased altogether to till the soil and thereafter depended purely on a pastoral economy, thus gaining increased mobility and the ability to seek refuge in the mountains in case of need. Archaeological evidence for the 5th century, however, has shown the error of this view : the material recovered points to the continuance of a settled population in the plains and to the persistence of the practice of agriculture — without which, in any event, the Latin vocabulary of agriculture could not have been preserved in the Romanian language. Nor were relations with the Roman world south of the Danube broken off ; and Roman or Romano-Byzantine products and coins continued to circulate north of the Danube and in the Carpathians. In this period some form of relationship must have been built up between the village communities and their Hunnic overlords, involving the appointment of a representative of the community for such purposes as fixing the amount of tribute to be paid and the form in which it was to be paid ; and accordingly we can assign to this period the beginnings of a system of production which can be called " tributary ".

Barbarian though it might be, the life of Attila's court was modelled on the Roman pattern, and the sources indicate that Latin was also spoken there. Moreover, as an abundance of archaeological evidence indicates, the material culture of Daco-Romania in the late 4th and the 5th centuries showed a revival — a renaissance — of Geto-Dacian, Roman and Romance traditions. This culture, with its distinctive characteristics, gave concrete expression to a restoration of the earlier unity, this time within a firmly established Romance framework. In this situation the domination of the Huns created favourable conditions for the maintenance of unity and for the establishment of relationships between the area of romanised culture in the Carpatho-Danubian region and the Roman world south of the Danube, i.e. the Empire. What we have called the " tributary " form of socio-economic structure represented a *modus vivendi* which benefited both the indigenous population and their Hunnic masters.

The culture of the period of Hunnic rule in Transylvania is known as the Bratei culture, on which we are well informed thanks to Ligia Bîrzu's monograph on cemetery No. 1 at Bratei. In the material from this site the

Roman element is predominant, but there are also features reflecting Geto-Dacian traditions as well as influences from the Sîntana de Mureş culture, now assimilated and integrated into the new Romance culture. There are also a number of other cemeteries and settlement sites dating from the same period in the former province of Dacia. In Moldavia, as in eastern Romania as a whole, this cultural entity is known as the Costişa culture, after the site of that name in the district of Neamţ, on which systematic excavation began in 1962. Similar material was found at Dodeşti (district of Galaţi), Crîngaşi (Bucharest), Ţaga (Cluj), Cipău (Mureş), Moreşti and other sites.

In the period when the Bratei-Costişa culture developed the population lived on river terraces or near sources of drinking water ; settlements on high ground were relatively rare. The pottery was either hand-made (in shapes following Dacian traditions) or wheel-turned. During the 6th century the pottery continued to develop in technique, form and ornament, but always on the basis of the 5th century types. The same Dacian and Roman traditions can be detected in the rites and rituals practised. One significant result emerged from the excavation of the La Tène cemetery at Ocniţa (Ocnele Mari) : the calcination of the graves observed in cemetery No. 1 at Bratei was practised by the Geto-Dacians before the conquest of Dacia, so that it is no longer necessary to explain the occurrence of this practice by supposing that it was transmitted by Illyrian settlers in Roman Dacia.

The economy of this period was based on agriculture, stock-rearing and craft production, indicating a stable and relatively prosperous population. In the tombs at Bratei, for example, large numbers of animal bones were found, no doubt representing offerings deposited in the tombs.

The end of the 4th century and the first half of the 5th are notable also for a series of rich treasures or grave deposits from princely tombs belonging to the leaders of the new dominant class which had established itself for the time being in the Carpatho-Danubian region. Typical of these is the famous treasure of Pietroasele (district of Buzău), an Ostrogothic hoard hidden during the troubled times following the death of Attila in 453 (K. Horedt). From the same period date the two treasures of Apahida and the treasures of Conceşti, Someşeni-Cluj *(Plates 119-121)* and Tăuteni-Bihor *(Plates 123, 124, 138).* The tomb of the Germanic chieftain Omharus at Apahida, which is dated to the second half of the 5th century, can be referred to the period of domination by the Gepidae after the death of Attila and the final defeat of the Huns. The contents of the princely tomb at Conceşti, now in the Hermitage Museum in Leningrad, appear to date from the same period as the Tăuteni material. The two treasures of Şimleul Silvaniei (district of Sălaj) have been dated to the 5th century. The treasure of Tăuteni, discovered in 1970, includes two silver gilt Romano-Byzantine vases, finely decorated, with inscriptions which have not yet been deciphered. Their repoussé decoration shows a different technique from the cloisonné work on the vases from Conceşti and Apahida, though these are of the same date (5th century) ; the ornamental motifs and the method of applying them belong to the Greco-Roman and Romano-Byzantine world. These various hoards or tomb deposits point to the transmission of the traditions and products of late antiquity through local channels to the chieftains of the migrant peoples, but they also bear witness to the glamour which Rome, and later Byzantium, still held for the migrant peoples. The exceptional richness of these hoards of precious metal and their high standard of artistic achievement demonstrate the stark contrast between the dominant position enjoyed by the possessors of such wealth and the poverty of the indigenous population, distinguished from the migrant peoples by a standard of material culture which was modest indeed but was based on ancient traditions. Of this contrast ample evidence has been provided both by the excavations of settlements and cemeteries and by chance finds throughout the area with which we are concerned.

CONTINUITY AND UNITY

VI

THE IPOTEŞTI-CÎNDEŞTI CULTURAL COMPLEX

The ethnic and cultural unity of the region with which we are concerned was, as we saw in the previous chapter, consolidated — this time on a Daco-Roman basis — in the 4th and 5th centuries. Although in its general structure this unity was found throughout the whole of the Carpatho-Danubian region, it represented a unity in diversity, since the culture took on different aspects in different parts of the region. But even the Hunnic invasions and the frequent periods of instability did not shake the cultural foundations of this unity or dissolve this local ethnic cohesion.

During the 5th, 6th and 7th centuries there is archaeological evidence of a cultural complex extending over a considerable geographical area which bears witness to the consolidation of this unity of Romance culture. This complex, known under the conventional designation of Ipoteşti-Cîndeşti — or sometimes, more comprehensively, Ciurelu (Bucharest) - Bratei - Moreşti (Transylvania) - Costişa - Botoşana (Moldavia) — has yielded the greatest abundance of material on the type sites. In 1974 Eugenia Zaharia attributed to the Ipoteşti-Cîndeşti complex a cremation cemetery at Sărata-Monteoru (district of Buzău), previously thought by Ion Nestor to be Slav, where intensive excavation between 1940 and 1958 brought to light no fewer than 1586 tombs. It is true that this large cemetery yielded items showing indigenous features, like pottery turned on a fast wheel (though this may have been merely an imitation of local ware), and Zaharia mentions the finding of an Early Christian glass object (a phylactery) and other items of indigenous origin. In the present author's view, however, the Sărata-Monteoru cemetery is mainly Slav, and the occurrence in this context of certain elements of non-Slav material and spiritual culture dating from the 6th and 7th centuries merely illustrates the process of contact, and later of symbiosis, between the native peoples and the Slavs which ended in the assimilation of the Slav incomers.

The Ipoteşti-Cîndeşti culture — taking the term in its archaeological acceptation — is now known throughout Romanian territory, and not only within the former Roman province of Dacia and round its borders. It is found, for example, on a number of sites within the boundaries of Bucharest (Străuleşti, Măicăneşti, Militari, Dămăroaia, Cernica, etc.), in Muntenia (Olteni, Sfinţeşti, Ipoteşti — on the left bank of the river Olt in the district of Olt — Tîrgşor-Prahova, etc.), in Moldavia (Botoşana-Bîtca-Oituz, Dodeşti, Costişa-Neamţ, Davideni, Tîrpeşti, Udeşti-Suceava, Curtea Domnească in the district of Bacău, etc.), in Transylvania (settlement No. 2 at Bratei — which shows continuity with the earlier period represented by settlement No. 1 and cemetery No. 1 — Bezid, settlement No. 1 at Poian, Filiaşi, etc.) and in Oltenia (Băbeni-Olteţ, Işalniţa, Stolniceni, Salcia, Gura Motrului, Craiova, etc.).

The archaeological evidence now available reflects the essentially Romance character of this complex and reveals its general unity of structure, but also presents certain local features resulting from varying degrees of romanisation and the greater or lesser impact of Geto-Dacian traditions. Geto-Dacian influence can be seen, for example, in the hand-made pottery, which in technique, form and decoration shows a reversion to the older tradition of domestically produced pottery.

Among distinctive features of the Ipoteşti-Cîndeşti complex are (1) open, unfortified settlements occupied by a sedentary population of farmers, stock-rearers and craftsmen ; (2) semi-subterranean huts, with hearths either dug out of the ground or edged with stone ; (3) hand mills of Roman type, consisting of a *meta* and a *catillus* ; (4) the fairly widespread practice of iron-working ; (5) slag and an iron bloom found at Budureasca, and agricultural implements from a number of other sites ; (6) items of personal adornment like the digitated fibulas which are fairly common, sometimes decorated with a cruciform motif, as in the example from Fărcaşele in the district of Olt, as well as silver or sometimes silver gilt ear-rings, pendants and bracelets ; (7) wheel-turned vases derived from Roman and Daco-

Roman prototypes of the 3rd and 4th centuries ; (8) a cruder type of hand-made pottery, some of the shapes being imitated from wheel-turned ware ; (9) cremation as the normal burial practice, with some instances of inhumation. In the inhumation burials (e.g. at Ceptura-Mizil in the district of Buzău, the basilica of Sucidava-Celei and the Insula Banului-Mehedinţi cemetery) we find a specifically Christian ritual, with the head to the west and the feet to the east. This co-existence of different burial practices is commonly met with in other areas during the early centuries of Christianity. The material found in the tombs also included some objects of Byzantine type, like ear-rings with star-shaped pendants in granulation work ; and significant in this connection also is the phylactery from the Sărata-Monteoru cemetery, which evidently belonged to a Christian member of the indigenous community and not to one of the Slav invaders.

The famous digitated fibulas formerly ascribed to the migrant peoples but now attributed to the Ipoteşti-Cîndeşti culture are characteristic of areas of essentially Romance stock. Moreover some of them, like the one from Fărcaşele, have the cross motif which points to the presence of Christians in the area. A number of moulds for casting crosses, dating from a rather later period, have been found : see below.

It is well established that the people of the Ipoteşti-Cîndeşti culture practised agriculture (as evidenced, for example, by the hand mills of Roman type), stock-rearing and metal-working. A number of local metal-working centres of the 6th and 7th centuries have been identified, for example within the area of Bucharest (Teodorescu, 1972). The material found on this site included crucibles, punches, chisels, moulds for ear-rings and crosses, ladles for pouring the molten metal, templates for pressing sheets of metal, etc. Another metal-working site at Budureasca-Mizil (district of Buzău) also produced objects reflecting local traditions as well as others of Romano-Byzantine type.

The settlements of this period, usually situated on low river terraces, attest the presence of a stable population which still had links with the Empire. All over the area of the Ipoteşti-Cîndeşti culture excavation has brought to light objects imported from the Romano-Byzantine world (for example jewellery and ornaments or amphoras, which were then imitated locally) and coins (see Map C, 6th and 7th centuries). Among coins commonly found are gold coins bearing the effigy of the Emperor Justinian, which penetrated deeply into Daco-Romania (being found, for example, in the districts of Vîlcea and Dîmboviţa).

The Ipoteşti-Cîndeşti culture was a phase of great historical importance in the life of the indigenous population. Its development extended over a considerable period, and the assimilation of numbers of disparate elements was a slow process. A unified structure was achieved, however, towards the end of the 6th century, and in the course of this development the foreign elements were successfully absorbed.

In the Carpatho-Danubian region the 6th century saw a return to more active relationships with the Empire. In the new conditions of the time, which represented a great change from earlier periods, the Romans sought to reassert their authority in the lower Danube area and to establish a buffer zone extending as deeply as possible into the territory north of the river. Justinian launched a number of expeditions over the Danube, rebuilt some of the earlier fortresses and constructed a number of new ones. From this period dates the rebuilding of the camps of Drobeta and Sucidava, among others.

The Christian remains dating from this period represent a cultural and spiritual horizon which enabled the area of Romance culture north of the Danube to maintain a steady process of development and consolidation, not only in virtue of its own dynamic force but also thanks to the protection of the Romano-Byzantine Empire and to the fact that the migrant peoples

116

stayed only for a limited time and in certain particular areas. This discontinuity of the migrants contrasted with the ethnic unity of the indigenous population and their settled way of life as farmers, stock-rearers and craftsmen.

THE GEPIDAE AND AVARS

In the 6th century we also find evidence in Transylvania of a Germanic culture — that of the Gepidae. The analysis by Kurt Horedt of the material from Moreşti, on the river Mureş, has thrown much new light on house types, technology, decorative styles in pottery and types of jewellery and ornament, and has made it possible to identify two distinct elements, one reflecting the Romance tradition and the other the Germanic traditions of the Gepidae. In the field of pottery, for example, there is clear evidence of the persistence into the 6th century of provision jars *(dolia)* of Daco-Roman type. We thus know that in some settlements the indigenous community lived side by side, on their own ancestral territory, with other more transient groups of Germanic origin.

The dominance of the Gepidae was maintained until another migrant people from Asia, the Avars, defeated them and established the beginnings of a system of political and military domination extending from the south-west of what is now the Soviet Union into Pannonia. The Avars also imposed their authority on groups of Gepidae who had settled on the territory of Romania. Evidence of their presence is provided by a number of important archaeological sites, like the Bratei cemetery, Noşlac, Moreşti and others in western Romania (Crişana) and in the south-west (the Banat). The Avars also left some traces of their passage in Oltenia ; but it is clear that the centre of their power was in western Romania and in the region between the Tisza and the Danube, where they were defeated by Charlemagne in 796. Characteristic of their material culture are their horse trappings and their weapons.

In an Avar tomb at Sînpetru German (district of Arad) was found a 7th century Byzantine gold coin with the effigies of the Emperor Heraclius and his son *(Plate 129)*, giving further evidence of the relationships between the Avars and Byzantium.

THE ADOPTION
OF CHRISTIANITY

VII

CHRISTIANITY AND THE LATIN LANGUAGE

At the beginning of the 4th century Constantine's Edict of Milan provided favourable conditions for the diffusion of the new faith of Christianity throughout the Roman Empire. The discovery of a whole series of Early Christian objects dating from the 4th century has provided information about the Daco-Romans living outside the bounds of the Empire. Among these objects, which must have reached the area immediately after the year 313, if not earlier, are a number of small Christian lamps *(lucernae)*, like the one found at Apulum (Alba Iulia). To the same period belongs the famous *donarium* of Biertan, in the district of Sibiu, with the Latin inscription *Ego Zenovius votum posui*, pointing to the existence of a place of worship on the site. It is also possible that a number of inhumation burials in Muntenia, with the heads to the west and the feet to the east, may have belonged to a local Christian community. The written sources record, too, that Christianity was preached among the Daco-Roman population north of the Danube by a number of missionaries, some speaking Latin and some Gothic.

Further evidence, also relating to this area in eastern Muntenia, is afforded by a document, of which little use has so far been made, giving an account of the martyrdom of St Sabas. The document in question is a letter sent from " Gothia " to the Christian church in Cappadocia when the saint's body was transported there, describing the circumstances in which he was drowned in the river Buzău on 12th April 372. The letter gives evidence of the close relationships between the Empire and the region north of the Danube, indicating that the Christian missionaries in this region were able to cross the river freely, and maintained close contact with the peoples south of the river, particularly with Scythia Minor. But the letter also brings out another significant fact. The river in which St Sabas was drowned was the Musaeus, from which the modern name Buzău derives. This is valuable evidence of the survival into our own day of the ancient name of one of the principal rivers in the region, which must undoubtedly have been preserved by the local population and taken over by the Germanic peoples.

Thus it is clear that in the 4th century Christianity was able to make headway both in the erstwhile province of Dacia and in the territory of the free Dacians, romanised in varying degrees, in which other peoples like the migrant Germanic tribes had temporarily established themselves. Undoubtedly, too, further archaeological work will supplement and enrich the evidence already available to us in this complex spiritual field.

Another significant fact, already noted, is the effort devoted by Justinian to the strengthening of the Danubian *limes*.

The excavations carried out over a number of years at Sucidava (Celei) led to the discovery of a Christian basilica, which not only demonstrated the general adoption of Christianity here but also pointed to the existence of an important centre with a hierarchy, an organisation and links with other communities both north and south of the Danube.

For the 6th century, and in the same territory south of the Carpathians, we have the evidence of a Christian bronze lamp from Luciu (district of Ialomiţa), on the left bank of the Borcea, with a cross on the handle *(Plate 128)*, which was reported by Vasile Pârvan as long ago as 1913. The evidence on the religious beliefs of the population of central Muntenia and Transylvania in this period is perhaps less adequate ; but we can cite in this connection the moulds for making crosses found in settlements of the indigenous population in Muntenia, which are dated by some scholars to the 6th century. It is significant that the moulds were found in huts capable of accommodating a considerable settled population.

A similar mould was found on a site in Bucharest (2 Str. Soldat Ghivan), another on a site at Bucharest-Străuleşti belonging to the Ciurelu-Ipoteşti-Cîndeşti cultural complex, and others again at Cîndeşti itself, associated with the same cultural complex, and at Olteni in central Muntenia. The finding of these moulds points not only to the presence of Christians in these areas but also to the existence of workshops producing the crosses to

101

TI·CLAVDIV[S]
[MA]XIMVS·VET[.]
[EQ]VES·MILITAVI[T]
[.]QV·INLEG·VIIC·P·F·[FA]
[C]TVS·QVI·STORIEQVIT[.]
SINGVLARIS·ETEGAT·ILL[.]
[E]CIONIS·HVS·DIE·M·VI·XII[.]
[H]ARIV·EQVITVM·ETEM[.]
[BE]LLO·DACICO·OB·VIRTV[.]
[I]I·DONIS·DONATVS·A·B[.]
[T]R·DOM·TIANO·FACTVS·DVPL[.]
ADIV·TROIANO·IN·ALA·SECV[.]
PANNONIORVM·A·QVO·ET·A[.]
[.]VS·EXPLORAT·OR·IN·BELLO·DA
CICO·ET·OB·VIRTVTE·BIS·DONIS
DONATVS·BELLO·DACICO·ET
PARTHICO·ET·AB·EODE·FACTV[.]
DECVRIO·IN·ALAE·ADE·QVOD
[C]EPISSET·DECEBALV·ET·CAP[.]
EIVS·PERTVLISSET·EI·RANIS·ST
ROMISSVS·VOLVNTARIVS·HO[.]
[H]ESTA·MISSIONE·ATERE[.]
[.]ARIO·CONSVLARE

102

[D]   M
[M]VC·A·TRA[.]
[.]RAS·I·MILE[S]
[I]N·BAL·MYREN[.]
[.]BISCENSIV[M]
[.]VIXIT·ANNIS·X[.]
[.]AVCA·POR·MVC[.]
[.]HERES·CON·TVB[.]
[.]ARISSI·M·Q·PO[.]

106

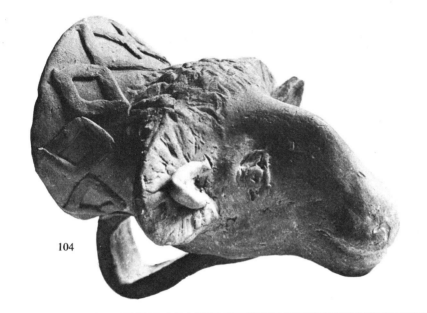

104

105

107

109

113

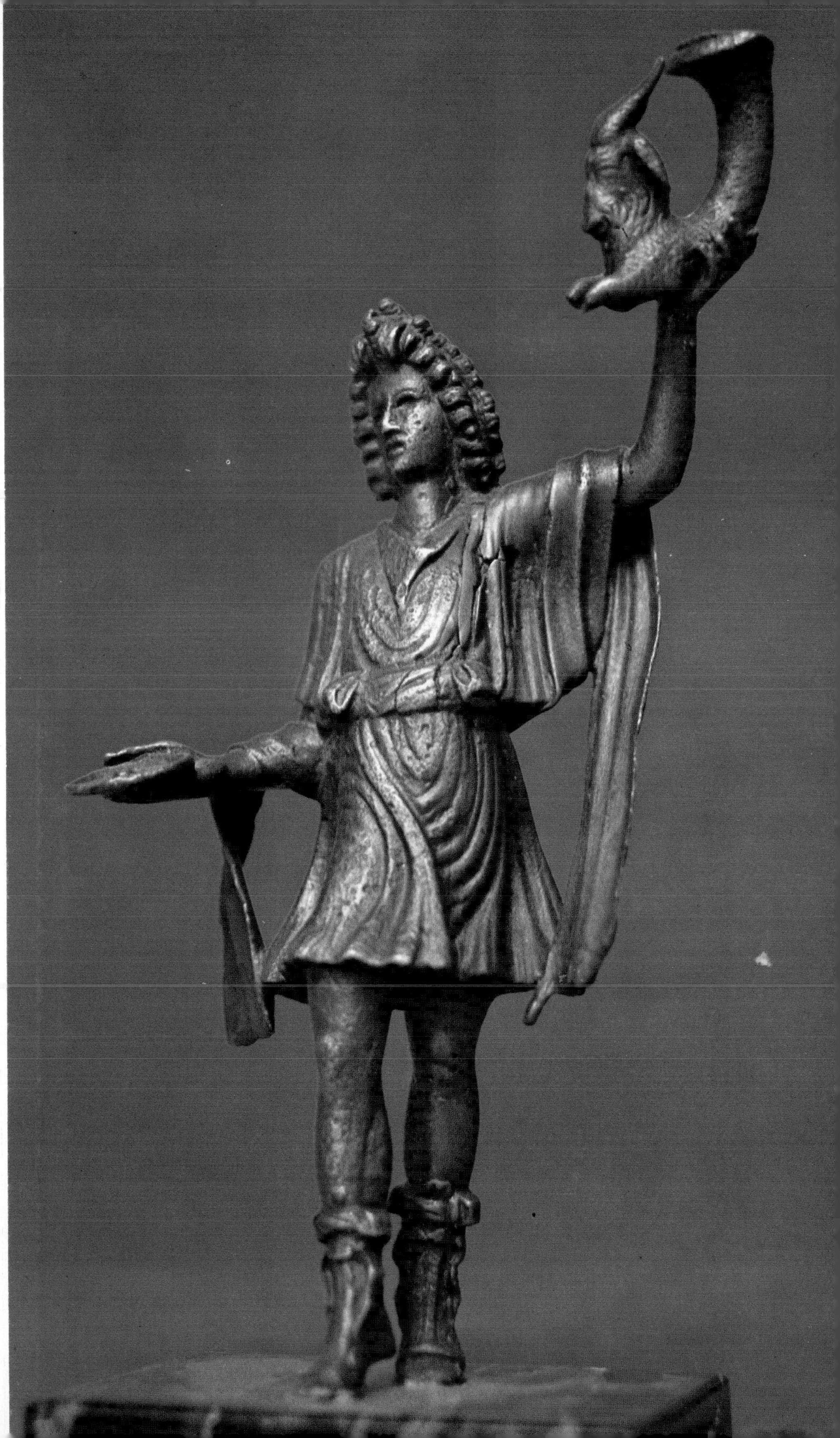

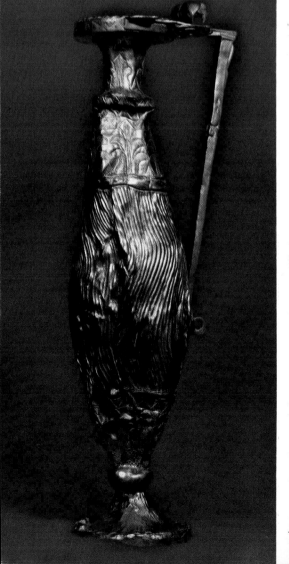

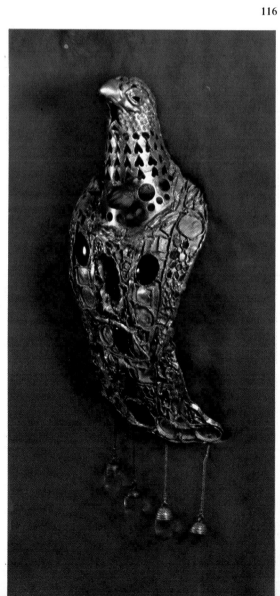

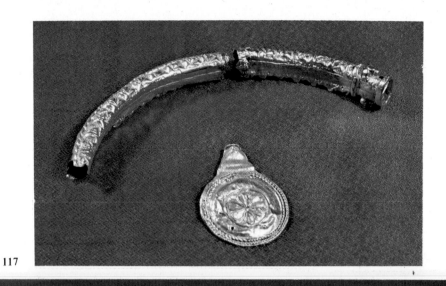

119

120

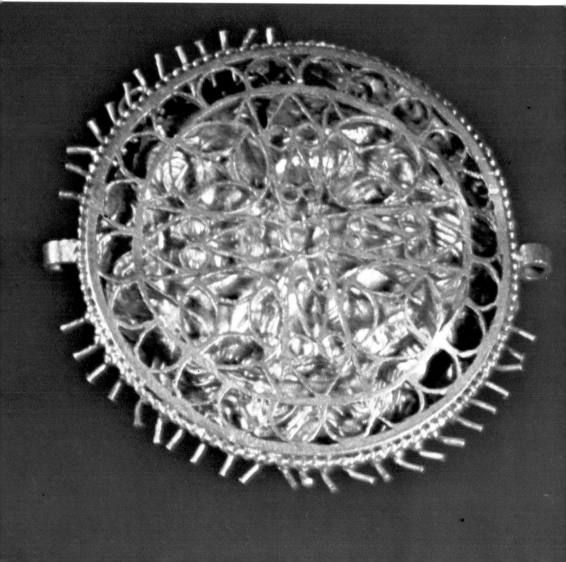

meet local demands. At Pîrjoaia in the Dobrudja, on the banks of the Danube, many crosses were found, also dated to the 6th century ; and their occurrence here seems to indicate that they were intended for export across the Danube. There is an abundance of similar evidence from all over the territory south of the Carpathians, from Oltenia into eastern Muntenia, in the hills no less than in the plains and on the banks of the Danube. For Transylvania we have the evidence of a Byzantine amphora, probably dating from the 6th century, recently discovered at Tîrgu Secuiesc (eastern Transylvania). On the upper part of the body, near the neck, is a painted cross with a Greek alpha and omega. The amphora was evidently imported from the Byzantine Empire for the use of a Christian community. Many similar vessels were found at Sucidava, and it is quite possible that they came from the entrepôt on the Danube — though they may also have come from somewhere in the Dobrudja by way of the Oituz pass. Also of interest in this connection is a small amphora with a painted cross from Luciu in the district of Ialomiţa. Finally from Tibiscum in the Banat we have an Early Christian vase which Constantin Daicoviciu dates to the 6th century.

Thus the evidence now available, both for the 4th and for the 6th century, shows that the romanised indigenous population, now properly called Proto-Romanian, were continuing to develop their spiritual life within a Christian framework over the whole territory of Romania. The archaeological evidence we have cited provides valuable corroboration of the linguistic evidence and facilitates its interpretation — for example in relation to the terms of Latin origin in the Romanian language expressing fundamental concepts associated with religious belief.

THE PROTO-ROMANIANS
AND THE SLAVS

VIII

During the final stage of its development the Ipoteşti-Cîndeşti-Botoşana-Bratei cultural complex came into contact with the Slavs, who entered the territory of Romania towards the end of the 6th century. The peoples belonging to this complex, culturally unified and of Romance character, were more numerous than the newcomers, they enjoyed a civilisation superior to that of the Slavs, and — an equally important factor — they formed part of a Romance linguistic unity which was then in process of crystallising. The coming of the Slavs did not dissolve this linguistic unity, extending as it did over the whole of the Ipoteşti-Cîndeşti culture, which, as we saw in Chapter VI, always had a Romance basis throughout its area of diffusion in the Carpatho-Danubio-Pontic region. Neither the fundamental vocabulary nor the syntax nor the morphology of the Romance language of the indigenous peoples was destroyed by the language of the Slavs, who were to live alongside the Proto-Romanian indigenous population for several centuries. In all the main fields of economic activity like agriculture, horticulture, vine-growing, milling, beekeeping and stock-rearing, in terms expressing family relationships (father, son, etc.) and in the names of the principal rivers like the Danube the Romanian language still preserves words of Latin origin in spite of the Slav influence to which it was exposed. The Slav phonetic system has affected the form of certain words, and terms of Slav origin have been accepted into the vocabulary to the extent of something like 16 per cent ; but 80 per cent of the vocabulary still consists of words of Latin origin which are in everyday use. (Of interest in this connection is B.P. Hasdeu's theory that the frequency of use of certain words gives a language its distinctive character).

THE EVOLUTION OF ROMANIAN LANGUAGE AND CULTURE

The archaeological evidence discussed in the preceding chapters, starting with the age-old unitary Thracian substratum, reflects the uninterrupted continuity of the material and spiritual culture of the indigenous population and the persistence over many centuries of certain forms of culture — first

Thraco-Geto-Dacian, then Daco-Roman and finally Romance. By dismembering the Germanic power structure — a process which was begun by the Huns — the Avar overlords, with the centre of their power in what is now Hungary, created conditions favourable to the indigenous population of Carpatho-Danubian Daco-Romania, and indeed reactivated Daco-Romania's relations with the Roman world south of the Danube.

It is well established that the Slav element did not play a predominant part in the ethnogenesis of the Romanian people and the formation of their language, though it exerted influence in both these fields. The results of linguistic, historical and archaeological study do not always agree in their assessment of the ethnic structure of a population or nation. In the particular case with which we are concerned linguistic analysis has proved that when the Slavs arrived the indigenous population spoke a language which was in process of crystallising. The Slavs were unable to destroy this language, but they added numerous words to its vocabulary and gave it a new and distinctive colouring. For this period the written sources contain only vague and sporadic references to the indigenous population of the Carpatho-Danubian region, although that population continued as before to live out their lives as farmers, stock-rearers and craftsmen. Thanks to the dynamic force of the migrant peoples — first Germanic, later Asiatic, but all transient and in constant movement — the settled population were brought into contact with new cultures ; but they in turn exerted an influence on the migrants which facilitated their integration into European civilisation and the assimilation for which they hankered of the heritage of the ancient world — results achieved during the formation of the barbarian states which grew up on the ruins of the Roman Empire.

The Slavs left a deeper imprint on the material culture of the Carpathians and the Danube region, and in this field their influence made itself felt more quickly and more positively than in the linguistic field. By the time they arrived, however, the formation of the Proto-Romanians was already an accomplished fact. The emergence of the Ipoteşti-Cîndeşti culture and the persistence of a Romance language structure after the coming of the Slavs show that by the late 6th and early 7th century the fundamental basis of the ethnic structure and the spiritual life of the Romanian people — their Romance character — was firmly established. With or without the Slav contribution, the ethnogenesis of the Romanians was bound to continue on the course on which it was already set ; though perhaps without the Slavs the process might have been completed more quickly and the earliest Romanian political structures might have appeared sooner.

Leaving speculation aside, however, the evidence now available makes it possible to assess the contribution of the Slavs on a proper scientific basis. The archaeological work of the last thirty years in eastern Romania, at such sites as Şipot-Suceava, Cucorăni-Botoşani, Hlincea I (Iaşi) and Dorobanţu, has revealed the presence of Slavs in this region at an early stage — as was indeed to be expected. On all these sites there is much Slav material, but always associated with local material : nowhere in Romania have any Slav settlements or cemeteries been found which do not show some influence from the local population. Even in the large Sărata-Monteoru cemetery, containing only cremation burials, which the present author is still inclined to regard as Slav, material characteristic of the Ipoteşti-Cîndeşti cultural complex was found, like the pottery turned on a fast wheel and decorated with wavy lines, fluting, ribbed patterns and narrow bands of hatching. Here too were discovered Christian objects which can have belonged only to the indigenous population. The first groups of Slavs who entered eastern Romania brought with them a material culture inferior to that of the local people. In Moldavia no purely Slav site has so far been discovered, indicating that as soon as they came into contact with the indigenous population the Slavs became involved in the process of interaction with the local culture which was to end in their assimilation. The local people continued with their own cultural development after the coming of the Slavs, just as their language continued to evolve in its own way. The first elements of Slav culture were discovered at Ciurelu, within the bounds of the present city of Bucharest, where the first archaeological evidence of the Ipoteşti-Cîndeşti complex was also found.

The Slavs then advanced west of the Olt ; but no purely Slav settlements have been found in Oltenia either. In the area between the Olt, the Danube and the Carpathians the Slavs who arrived at the end of the 6th century and remained there in subsequent centuries developed the same pattern of co-existence with the local population. Even on sites which are accepted as Slav, like the cemetery of Balta Verde (district of Mehedinţi), Byzantine material is also found.

Towards the end of the 6th century the presence of the Slavs is also attested by archaeological evidence in south-eastern Transylvania, always an area through which connections between the two sides of the Carpathians were maintained, and in the migration period much used by the migrant peoples as a route for their onward passage or as a temporary halting place. Excavations carried out by Z. Székely of Sf. Gheorghe between 1960 and 1970 recovered Slav material at Cernat and Poian (district of Covasna), and material dating from the same period was found at Porumbenii Mici (district of Harghita), Bratei (district of Sibiu), Dorolţu-Cluj (cemeteries), Ocna Mureş and other sites. The tumulus burials at Nuşfalău (Sălaj) and Someşeni (Cluj) have always been attributed to the Slavs, but they are of later date and yielded objects of Avar workmanship. It has to be remembered also that in spite of the considerable amount of Slav archaeological material this density of settlement is not confirmed by the linguistic evidence (though there are a certain number of Slav place-names).

DEVELOPMENT OF THE PROTO-ROMANIANS

The crossing of the frontier of the Byzantine Empire on the Danube in 602 was the prelude to further advances by ever larger groups of Slavs, who surged over the river and continued through the romanised territory in the Danubio-Balkan region to reach Greece and the Adriatic. This southward move was advantageous to the development of the population north of the Danube, which would otherwise have been stifled by the weight of Slav pressure. The unity of the Balkans was now destroyed ; but the Thracian and Romance substratum still served as a link with the region north of the Danube and acted as a revivifying force when the Byzantine Empire again extended its authority up to the Danube in the 10th and 11th centuries. Communications between the two sides of the river were now easier, and the Proto-Romanian nucleus in the Danubian region was thus strengthened.

In the 7th and 8th centuries the archaeological evidence for the material culture of the Carpatho-Danubian region shows a speeding up in the pace of assimilation of the Slavs and the steady development of a material and spiritual culture of fundamentally Romance — and, more specifically, Proto-Romanian — character. The pottery types are increasingly varied, with a decoration of wavy lines and hatching ; the hand-modelled vases are ornamented with pitting and incisions. Important material belonging to this period, including both products imported from the Byzantine world and objects made in local workshop, has been found at Bezid, Sălaşuri, Filiaşi, Eliseni (Harghita) and other sites. The wheel-thrown pottery preserves Roman and Daco-Roman traditions. In Moldavia too we can follow the development of the local Proto-Romano-Slav culture in the archaeological material of the 7th, 8th and 9th centuries. The diffusion of coins (Map C) also illustrates the links between this region and the Byzantine territory to the south.

Further evidence of the Slav element during these centuries is provided by the material recovered at Lozna, Fundu Herţii (district of Botoşani) and Dolheşti-Vaslui. At Poiana-Dulceşti (district of Neamţ) and Sălişte excavations by G. Bichir revealed a horizon dating from the 8th century (first and second half of the century respectively). In Oltenia evidence on the 8th century has been provided both by chance finds and by excavation of settlement sites and cemeteries. The most important of these sites is the Obîrşia Nouă cemetery, which the excavator, O. Toropu, dated "provisionally" to the 8th century and the first quarter of the 9th. Comparative material has been supplied by the Izvoru-Ilfov cemetery, in the area formerly known as Vlaşca — a Slav name meaning "land of the Romanians".

During the 7th and 8th centuries the Carpatho-Danubian and Balkan region was in a permanent state of instability. On one side were the Avars, on the other the Slavs, some of them free and others subject to the Avars. Then about the final decades of the 7th century the Proto-Bulgarians appeared on the scene, under the command of their military leader Asparuch or Isperich, and after defeating the Byzantines established themselves in the north-east of present-day Bulgaria, with Pliska and Preslav as their capitals. Here they settled among the Slavs who had begun to move south of the Danube in large numbers in 602. This region was inhabited by a Romance population whom the Slavs had not succeeded in assimilating, or even in breaking up into small separate units — a result not achieved until the first Bulgarian kingdom or kaganate. This considerable indigenous population therefore continued for the time being to co-exist with the newcomers and with the Slavs who had long occupied the Balkano-Danubian region ; and elements deriving from this population can still be detected in Bulgarian culture, art and folk traditions. The Bulgars themselves — who were in any event of mixed ethnic composition — were assimilated by the Slavs and adopted their Slavonic language, while preserving their own name.

Our knowledge of the period of Proto-Bulgarian domination north of the Danube is very imperfect. Within the territory of Romania itself we have some material belonging to the Proto-Bulgarian culture which may have been brought there either by the Proto-Bulgarians themselves, by the Slavs or by the Proto-Romanians. But in spite of the prevailing instability and insecurity — which led to the stowing away of hoards of valuable objects like the one found at Priseaca (district of Olt) dating from the second half of the 7th century — the indigenous population still remained on the land inhabited by their ancestors.

THE IZVORU CEMETERY

The archaeological work of the last few years has greatly enlarged our knowledge of the culture of the 8th century. Of particular significance in this respect is the recently discovered cemetery at Izvoru, near Giurgiu, with both inhumation and cremation burials, which throws light on the material and spiritual culture of this period. Up to 1973 a total of 432 tombs had been excavated, mostly inhumation burials with the head to the west and the feet to the east. In the less numerous cremation burials the bones, broken and thoroughly burned, were deposited in simple pits.

The inhumation tombs contained a variety of offerings, together with objects of personal adornment. The offerings included a number of implements, most significantly perhaps sickles, which were found in three tombs. These implements show beyond any possibility of doubt that the main occupation of the inhabitants was agriculture ; and this was confirmed by the finding in some tombs of carbonised grain, deposited either in a pottery vessel or round the dead person's head. The offerings also included large quantities of animal bones from poultry, cattle and sheep, as well as numerous birds' eggs.

Among other objects found in the tombs were pottery vessels, usually placed at the dead person's feet, and iron knives, placed under the palm of either the right or the left hand. The knives were found in tombs belonging to either men, women or children.

The objects of personal adornment included ear-rings, finger-rings and necklaces of coloured glass paste beads. Some tombs contained bone tubes

144

for iron needles and iron or bronze buckles. Detailed study of the ear-rings and finger-rings, sickles and a bronze applied ornament and analysis of their form and decoration make it possible to date the cemetery mainly to the 8th century. The iron and bronze buckles take its beginnings back to the 7th century ; its final stage overlaps into the 9th.

Analysis of the personal ornaments, with particular reference to the metal of which they are made, leads to certain conclusions about social structure. The greater richness of certain tomb deposits, consisting of several dozen items of silver jewellery, compared with others consisting of larger numbers of bronze objects and with three tombs containing bronze bracelets, points to some degree of social differentiation among the inhabitants of Izvoru.

The Izvoru cemetery also suggests certain more general conclusions about the people of Romania during this period. In the first place the large number of burials (no fewer than 432 by the end of 1973) indicates the considerable size of the population. We know also that the population was settled and organised, and that it was beginning to show divisions between different economic and social categories ; and we know that its principal activities were farming and stock-rearing.

The Izvoru cemetery is by no means unique. Similar cemeteries have been brought to light in Romania within the last few years, particularly in the area between the Carpathians and the Danube — for example at Frǎteşti (district of Ilfov) and Obîrşia Nouǎ in Oltenia and Sultana in Muntenia. This archaeological evidence demonstrates the existence in southern Romania, between Ialomiţa and Jiu, of a stable indigenous population. The orientation of the bodies and the various Christian objects found at Obîrşia Nouǎ make it clear that this population was Christian. The same popu-lation is found, though so far with more limited archaeological evidence, in Moldavia (excavations by I. Mitrea) and Transylvania (excavations by Z. Székely).

THE HISTORICAL SIGNIFICANCE OF THE EIGHTH CENTURY HORIZON

The application of demographic methods to archaeology by Romanian specialists in this field has revealed a fairly large number of settlements and cemeteries in Oltenia, in addition to chance finds. Some 20 sites (Balta Verde, Fărcaşul de Sus, Verbiţa, Obîrşia Nouă, etc.) are known for the 8th century, and 24 for the 9th. The material recovered points to a large and stable Romanian population with an advanced culture and economy. It was of the Christian faith ; it was heir to Roman and Daco-Roman traditions ; it was equipped with implements for the practice of agriculture and had its own craftsmen ; and it still maintained its economic links with the regions south of the Danube.

Of the cemeteries associated with this population the largest and the best known, following systematic excavation by O. Toropu, is the one at Obîrşia Nouă, where up to the end of 1973 a total of 105 tombs had been found (95 with inhumation burials and 10 with cremations). The material found in this cemetery provided concrete evidence of the presence of an indigenous Christian population in the area.

The Izvoru-Obîrşia Nouă cultural complex also extended to other Romanian provinces. Ethnically it was clearly Romanian, though with a Slav element which was well on the way to assimilation by the indigenous population.

THE EIGHTH AND NINTH CENTURIES

IX

THE DRIDU CULTURE

The Balkano-Danubian or Dridu culture, found in Romania and neighbouring countries, is characterised by a type of fine pottery, brownish black or grey in colour with a decoration of brilliantly coloured lines, a white or red-painted ware, amphoras, a cruder type of pottery with a high proportion of sand in the fabric, and a group of glazed ware. The culture is usually dated to the 8th-11th centuries, but an earlier stage is also distinguished which may go back to the late 7th or early 8th century. Its area of diffusion lay south of the Carpathians, reaching down into the Balkans. So far material belonging to this culture has been found at a number of sites in southern and south-eastern Transylvania, including Blandiana, Sebeş, Poian, Coşeni (where Kurt Horedt carried out excavations in 1973) and the cemeteries of Sebeş and Ocna Sibiului. The same culture is also found in eastern Romania. Its ethnic attribution is still matter for argument, particularly since only sporadic evidence of this culture has so far been found north of the Carpathians in the former Roman province of Dacia. It is probable that the population embraced by this culture belonged to more than one ethnic group, since one culture can absorb others. We do not yet know enough about the culture to distinguish either purely local variations or differences peculiar to larger areas.

The Dridu culture is found in fully developed form in the 10th and 11th centuries. The horizon represented by the large cemetery at Izvoru (see Chapter VIII) and the Obîrşia Nouă cemetery in Oltenia (with a considerable quantity of Christian material which can be attributed only to the indigenous population) undoubtedly casts a new light on the genesis and ethnic affinities of the Dridu culture; but the problem requires detailed study by both Romanian and Bulgarian archaeologists, who may find in the Izvoru-Obîrşia Nouă horizon answers to some of the questions which puzzle them about the rather heterogeneous structure of the Dridu culture and the contributions made to its formation by its various constituent elements.

The Dridu culture came into being on the basis of a common stock of Romance and Thraco-Geto-Daco-Roman ethno-cultural traditions. The archaeological material recovered in Transylvania, though still limited in quantity, has thrown further light on this common stock. Another major factor was the Slav element, which spread like a flood over the whole of the Carpatho-Danubio-Balkan and Pontic region (see next chapter), apparently overwhelming the Romance material culture of this whole territory. The third factor, and one of considerable importance, was Byzantine. Clearly, too, account must be taken of the Oriental influence which was first brought in by the Bulgars and later continued to operate through the survival in this region of cultural traditions inherited from other migrant peoples of Asiatic and Germanic stock. These peoples stayed for some time in the lower Danube region and the Dobrudja, in isolated groups, and are believed to have played a significant part in the evolution of the pottery known as Dridu ware and the pottery of Saltovo-Mayatsk type found in the Crimea and the Sea of Azov region. Finally consideration must be given to the contribution made by Greek culture — a term to be taken here in its widest connotation and not merely in the sense of Byzantine or Romano-Byzantine. When we are able to determine with some confidence the proportion in which these various factors contributed to the genesis of the Dridu culture and the consequential emergence of certain regional peculia- rities mainly determined by these factors, it will be possible to distinguish more clearly the results of the process of ethnic polarisation which took place under the superimposed Slav layer of population — a " population nappe " in the sense discussed in the following chapter.

As to the name of this culture, the present author is disposed to accept the term Carpatho-Balkan recently suggested by the young Romanian archaeologist O. Toropu in place of the older designation of Dridu or Balkano-Danubian culture. The term Carpatho-Danubio-Balkan might be even more apt, since the Danube formed the axis of its area of diffusion. The river also represented an important linking factor from the cultural, historical and ethnic point of view, for the Pontic region was also within the compass of this culture, as is shown by the archaeological material recovered at Histria-Sat, Satu Nou, Castelu, Gîrliţa and other sites.

North of the Danube and in the Carpathians, as in the Dobrudja, it was the Romance and Proto-Romanian elements and traditions that were predominant; Slav elements were also present but were less prominent. South of the Danube, in what is now Bulgaria, the Slav element was overwhelmingly in the ascendant: after the year 602 the Slavs thrust into this region on a massive scale, established themselves in compact groups and assimilated — linguistically, culturally and biologically — the Turkic Bulgars or Proto-Bulgarians. North of the Danube the indigenous population were unable to hold out for any length of time in their fortified settlements, although the term *sat* (from the Latin *fossatum*) bears witness to the existence of such settlements after the year 271 and, as we have already noted, provides evidence of linguistic continuity in the Romanian language, which in turn reflects an ethnic continuity.

The houses of this period were rectangular in plan, or sometimes huts of simpler type, with hearths. The rituals practised reflect Geto-Dacian, Daco-Roman and provincial Roman traditions (these last inherited from Roman settlers, soldiers and officials), as well as certain Slav traditions. Imports from the Byzantine world and the re-establishment of Byzantine authority over the Danube and a strip of territory along the left bank in the 10th and 11th centuries reactivated the old Roman cultural stock and promoted the revival of earlier traditions. Progress was made between the 8th and 10th centuries in the development of agriculture, stock-rearing and the various crafts. Evidence of this is provided, for example, by the excavations at Bîrlogu (district of Argeş), the site of a village in which more than 450 houses were brought to light. Here I. Nania found a hoard of objects near a craftsman's workshop, together with an iron plough and a brick bearing an inscription in Proto-Bulgarian runes. Similar finds were made at Slon by Maria Comşa.

It is interesting to note the persistence of Christian archaeological material in the Carpatho-Danubio-Pontic cultural horizon which developed on the basis of the Ipoteşti-Cîndeşti complex. This persistence demonstrates that both in the 8th century and later the population was Christian, sedentary and Romanian. We have already observed that certain 8th century cemeteries, like the one at Obîrşia Nouă, contained considerable quantities of Christian objects which must have belonged to the indigenous Romanian population. It is of significance also that soon after the middle of the 9th century (864-865) the Bulgars adopted Christianity under Tsar Boris I.

Thus the unity of the large Carpatho-Histro-Pontic and Balkan cultural complex, with which was associated the area of the Saltovo-Mayatsk culture to the north-east, concealed a number of different ethnic elements — Romanian, Bulgarian, Slav — each predominating in a particular area but involved in contact and interchange with the others.

It is well known to archaeologists that a material culture does not always coincide with a particular ethnic unit ; and the cultural complex we have been considering offers a striking example of this. Throughout Daco-Romania this culture belonged to the Romanians, who in the Ipoteşti-Cîndeşti phase were at the stage which can be defined as Proto-Romanian. The assimilation of the Slavs began in the late 6th and early 7th century. Within the territory of Daco-Romania — in which we must include the whole of the extensive territory covered by the unitary Geto-Dacian and Daco-Roman culture — this process took place in a rural setting, within the framework of a village economy : a milieu which is always conservative, disposed to cling to tradition, attached to the land of its ancestors. The " masters of the land ", particularly those who lived in the modest villages of the tumultuous migration period, were able to maintain the continuity of spiritual and cultural life in which the genesis of the Romanian people took place.

EMERGENCE OF THE ROMANIAN PEOPLE

The last migrants into the extra-Carpathian region had no effect on the ethnic and cultural unity of the indigenous population, and indeed were unable even to establish a settlement in the area.

North of the Danube, within the Carpatho-Histro-Pontic cultural area, there were in the 10th century a number of well established settlements under local chieftains, mentioned in the written sources, which (according to P. Diaconu) submitted to the Emperor John Tzimisces after Svyatoslav's surrender in 971. Nor were the Pechenegs able to destroy or even to supplant the indigenous culture : by this time the Romanian people had crystallised and now formed a compact bloc. Certain Pecheneg elements survived in the culture and organisation of the region, just as at a later period Pecheneg features were transmitted by the Cumans and Tartars. But the successive waves of migrants were powerless to halt the continuing development of the ancient culture of Romania. The archaeological evidence on this point is quite unequivocal ; and Romanian unity was preserved not only in the field of material culture, on which excavation has thrown so much light, but also in the language, with its absence of dialectal variations.

ASSIMILATIONS AND SURVIVALS

X

" POPULATION NAPPES " AND CENTRES OF POLARISATION

In Nicolae Iorga's view the existence of a single substratum throughout the Carpatho-Histro-Pontic region — which he regarded as extending over the rest of the territory south of the Danube — was a factor of capital importance which maintained the unity of the Romanian people during the 7th-8th and later centuries, until the emergence of the political formations which preceded the establishment of regular states.

This substratum continued to develop and preserved its full vitality even during the migration period, when it was submerged by successive waves of incomers. Borrowing a term from geology, we can describe these alien overlays as " population nappes " — intrusive layers thrust over the existing substratum. The cultural unity of the substratum was maintained, but through a process of polarisation round a number of different centres a series of variations developed within the overall unity, for example in the 4th-5th and 6th-7th centuries. Thus we find in the indigenous culture — as in the earlier Geto-Dacian culture and indeed in the cultures of the preceding millennia — the phenomenon of unity in diversity which is illustrated in concrete and eloquent form by the archaeological evidence. The passage of the migrant peoples, bringing their own cultures with them, accentuated these local particularisms without destroying the fundamental unity of structure. During the period of development and diffusion of the Sîntana de Mureş-Chernyakhov culture the Goths threatened to submerge the unitary local culture when they adopted a form of settled life and showed signs of establishing themselves permanently ; but the arrival of the Huns, who came into conflict with the Germanic peoples and put a halt to their encirclement of the indigenous population, enabled the local culture to recover the freedom it had enjoyed in the past, even in the areas where native cultural patterns and biological forces had been absorbed into the Sîntana de Mureş-Chernyakhov culture.

126

125

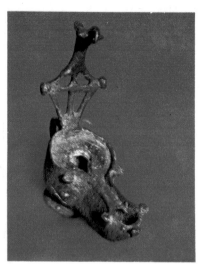

128

129

130

131

132

133

134

135

136

137

138

The resurgence of the secular unity of the indigenous culture which now took place may appear surprising, but it is well attested by archaeological evidence all over the area. During the nominal domination of the Huns, as a result of their close links with the Empire and the adoption of a Roman way of life by the Hunnic chieftains under Attila's command, we observe the re-establishment of the earlier cultural unity of the Geto-Dacian and Daco-Roman periods, but now in the form of the cultural horizon of the 4th and 5th centuries. The Hunnic domination also had a positive side, establishing more favourable conditions for a return to the old forms of economic, social and spiritual life. The pressure exerted by the Huns thrusting forward from the east not only led to a rapid withdrawal by the Goths — who soon afterwards, in the first quarter of the 5th century, also abandoned Transylvania — but also served to facilitate the continued process of fusion between the former free Dacians (in this case the Daco-Carpi) and the romanised population. When the Huns established themselves in Pannonia and from there launched their raids of intimidation and plunder they again promoted the regrouping of the former free Dacians in the western part of the old Roman province and their union with the romanised population of the interior. The ethnic and cultural unity of the region was now consolidated. The defeat and withdrawal of the Gepidae and later of the Avars also contributed to the destruction of the superimposed " population nappe " which overlay the indigenous population and threatened to stifle them. The archaeological material belonging to the migrant peoples is different from that of the " old-established indigenous peoples, firmly attached to the land and engaged in tilling the soil, herding and stock-rearing " (I. Andrieşescu).

The Slavs in turn covered the indigenous population of the Carpatho-Histro-Pontic region — the territory of Daco-Romania — with a population nappe varying in density from one area to another. When the Slavs arrived Daco-Romania formed an ethnic and cultural unity which is known to us in the 6th and 7th centuries in the form of the Ipoteşti-

Cîndeşti cultural complex. In these areas the Slavs found in being a series of local areas of romanised culture — groups of village communities whose Geto-Dacian and Daco-Roman traditions had been preserved under the overlying nappe formed by the military ruling class of the migrant peoples. Links between the local population and the incomers were provided by representatives of the village communities whose function was to arrange for the collection of the tribute which these communities had to pay, in various forms, to their temporary overlords. There were thus three elements in this " tributary " system of production — the alien ruling class, the local communities and the representatives of those communities who acted as go-betweens. Thanks to the work of Miron Constantinescu we know something of the operation of this system in the period of the earliest political formations in Romania, which are attested in the written sources ; but it was already in existence, though perhaps in a simpler form, in the early migration period. At any rate it is well established that the passage of so many peoples over the territory of Romania directly ensured the existence, the permanence and the continuity of the Romanian people, as Constantinescu has recently observed.

The Slavs found an indigenous population speaking a Romance language, and gave them the name of Vlahi, which they had taken over from the Germanic peoples. This population was grouped in indigenous village communities or *vlahii*, with their own organisation. In Nicolae Iorga's view these *vlahii* corresponded to the earlier *romaniae*, centres of polarisation of Thraco-Roman, Geto-Roman, Daco-Roman and finally Romanian culture — ethnic groups living in coherent geographical units (a river valley, an area of forest, etc.). Ethnic groupings of this kind were known to the Slavs ; and Iorga was the first to observe the resemblance between the *shchei* of the Slavs and the *romaniae* and *vlahii* of Romania or the similar Cuman communities of a later period. Organisations of this kind did not, of course, exist wherever there were settlements of the indigenous or the migrant peoples, but only where this phenomenon of polarisation or concentration had occurred. In both archaeological and and demographic studies, therefore, it is necessary to take account of the geographical situation of settlements, cemeteries and tombs, and the hoards deposited by the migrant peoples, as well as river-names and place-names.

In the Teleorman area a Turanian population was able to maintain itself for some time, and to the west of this area was the centre of polarisation of the Romanian " land of the *vlahii*" (Vlăsia). In other areas there were centres of polarisation of the Slavs, who had from the outset been exposed to cultural influences from the Romanian population which was in process of assimilating them. It is perhaps legitimate, therefore, to assign the treasure of Sînnicolau Mare (district of Timiş, Banat), probably dating from the 9th century, to the period when the assimilation of the Slavs was taking place in the Slav or Slavo-Bulgarian area of polarisation in the Banat.

It thus appears that the theory of population nappes put forward by the Romanian historian P.P. Panaitescu may be confirmed by the evidence on the migration period brought to light by the archaeological work of the last thirty years. Panaitescu was concerned only with the Slav nappe and with the Romanian nappe, which has also been considered recently by the young Romanian historian A. Armbruster (1972) with reference to the Dridu culture.

In the present author's view the archaeological evidence allows us to conclude that population nappes of this kind existed throughout the migration period over areas of varying extent, that there was frequently a process of interpenetration between them, and that the nappes formed by the migrant peoples down to the time of the Slavs were relatively thin and short·lived, being rapidly blown away by the wind of history.

The existence of the *romaniae*, the *vlahii* and a number of centres of polarisation of the migrant peoples — some of which, particularly but not exclusively those of the Slavs, may have lasted for some time — seems to suggest that there is a case for linking the theory of population nappes with the concept of centres of polarisation (i.e. areas showing a higher than average concentration within a population containing different ethnic groups). It is significant that linguists who have studied the formation of the Romanian language, among them Gamillscheg and Reichenkron, have drawn attention to linguistic *Kerngebiete* of this kind.   A. Philippide noted " traces of Roman culture " among Romanians living in the Apuseni Mountains, making them appear much older than the alien peoples who had penetrated into Transylvania.

It is clear that the denser Slav nappe in the region south of the Danube was able in the 8th-10th centuries to stifle and assimilate the Proto-Bulgarians and the Moeso-Geto-Romance population.   In Greece, however, the Slav nappe was so thin that the Slavs themselves were rapidly assimilated. North of the Danube, in Daco-Romania, this Slav nappe was relatively durable, with certain centres where the Slav element was denser, and was able to maintain itself longer — but only in these particular areas.   The archaeological evidence shows that in the 6th and 7th centuries the Proto-Romanians were victorious in their linguistic and cultural confrontation with the Slavs.   The process which was set in motion when the Slavs arrived in Daco-Romania in the 8th century culminated in the assimilation of the Slavs and the consummation of the final stage in the ethnogenesis of the Romanian people.   This development took place over the whole of Romanian territory.   The cultural and ethnic permanence derived from the Thracian substratum emerges clearly from the recent archaeological evidence, as illustrated in this volume.   Even though we still find references in the Byzantine, Magyar and Russian sources to Slavs and Slavo-Romanians, and not merely to Romanians, this does not alter the established fact that the Romanian people and their language were fully formed by the 8th century, having developed out of the earlier stage represented in the 6th and 7th centuries by the Proto-Romanians.

CONCLUSION

The archaeological material illustrating this history of Daco-Romania is taken so far as possible from recent excavations by Romanian archaeologists, not only those attached to universities and other academic institutions but also those working in the numerous district museums throughout Romania which are active local centres of archaeological and historical research.

The remarkable results achieved by archaeology in Romania have demonstrated the importance of the Thracian substratum, the starting point of this study. This played a fundamental part in securing the persistence, unity and continuity of later ethno-cultural syntheses and provided the basis on which these successively developed until the ethnogenesis of the Romanian people and the formation of their language were successfully accomplished.

Within the geographical and historical framework of Daco-Romania itself this substratum preserved its full vigour and remained perennially active, serving as a ferment whose beneficial effects were felt throughout the whole Carpatho-Danubio-Pontic region. In the other areas south of the Danube where the Thracian substratum existed, particularly in Bulgaria, it manifested itself only in the persistence of Thracian traditions, since in these areas it was disturbed and displaced by the massive Slav penetration from the year 602 onwards and later by the arrival of the Proto-Bulgarians. Nevertheless some traces of this substratum can still be detected in the territory south of the Danube.

It was in Daco-Romania, however, that a unitary ethnic and cultural synthesis, showing perfect continuity of development, came into being on the basis of the Thracian substratum. The process is well documented by the archaeological evidence illustrated and discussed in this volume. To the material already available we are now able to add the first inscriptions in the Thraco-Dacian language, discovered at Ocniţa in 1973, along with the bronze mask illustrated in *Plate 48*. We are happy to give readers of the " Archaeologia Mundi " series an early opportunity of seeing this recent find of such outstanding importance and interest.

The archaeological evidence gives us a clear picture of the unity of the material and spiritual culture of the Geto-Dacians throughout the area stretching from the northern slopes of the Balkans to the northern Carpathians and extending over a considerable distance from east to west. Within this wide territory the Geto-Moesians and the Getae belonged to a single ethnic and cultural whole.

The development of Geto-Dacian culture proceeded at different rates, more rapidly in the Histro-Pontic region and at a slower pace in the intra-Carpathian provinces of Romania.   Unity of material and spiritual culture and linguistic unity were, however, permanently maintained, the unifying force in Geto-Dacian times being derived directly from the earlier Thracian unity.

The Roman thrust into the Balkans and the extension of their authority to the Danube in the time of Augustus represented a new development whose repercussions were felt not only in the political, military and linguistic fields but also in material culture ; and the ethno-cultural unity of the Geto-Dacians was damaged and weakened when the Geto-Moesian region was severed from the rest of their territory and incorporated in the Roman Empire.

We have shown the creative way in which Geto-Dacian culture absorbed features from other cultures — Greek, Celtic and Roman. Our interpretation of the archaeological evidence leads to the conclusion that the assimilation of many elements of Greek civilisation and the establishment of close economic links with Greece — indicated by the diffusion of imports from the Greek world and the circulation of Greek and Hellenistic coins among the Geto-Dacians — promoted the process of romanisation, since Greek civilisation had of course a profound influence on the structure of Roman civilisation. The Celtic heritage, the influence of which is perceptible particularly in western Romania, also had a part to play in this process, since it had already exerted its beneficial and enriching influence on the Romans.

Thus the romanisation of the Geto-Dacians did not take place within a province of the barbarian world. Daco-Romania stemmed on the one hand from the Thracian substratum, with traditions reaching back for many millennia, and from the unitary Geto-Dacian culture, but on the other from a civilisation which had also contributed much to Roman civilisation. The archaeological work of the last 25 or 30 years in Romania has shown that Roman influence north of the Danube, reflected in concrete form by the penetration of Roman imports and Roman coins, went much deeper and started much earlier than had previously been thought, antedating by more than a century and a half the conquest of Dacia by Trajan. The recent discoveries at Ocniţa in north-eastern Oltenia — where there are rich deposits of salt which were worked by both the Dacians and the Romans — have shown that in the time of Augustus the Geto-Dacians knew the Latin alphabet and used it to write their own Thraco-Dacian language *(Plate 80)*, and that in the time of Decebal (cf. the pottery stamps from Sarmizegetusa) they could write and understand Latin. Roman coins of the Republican period were taken as the model for the new Dacian coinage which replaced the coins issued by tribal confederations before the 1st century B.C. Moreover the recent archaeological discoveries in Daco-Romania south and east of the Carpathians have shown the degree of control already exercised by the Romans and the deep cover zone they maintained on the north bank of the Danube.

The novelty of the present volume, as compared with the earlier volume on Romania published in 1972, lies in the fuller knowledge now available of the process of romanisation in every field of life, the early beginnings of the process, its persistence after 271, the wide territory over which it took place (extending considerably beyond the Roman province of Dacia) and the important part played by the lower Danube region — the river forming a permanent and active zone of contact between the population of Daco-Romania and the Roman world south of the Danube. The picture we now have is very different from that of a " Scythian " pattern of romanised culture.

Another new feature, linked with the wider definition of Daco-Romania, is the rôle of the free Dacians as it is now understood : a rôle of decisive importance in maintaining Thraco-Geto-Daco-Roman continuity on the basis of the earlier unity of the region and in re-establishing the ethno-cultural unity of the whole Carpatho-Danubian and Pontic region after 271. The free Dacians themselves became involved in the process of romanisation, though with much local differentiation, since the scale and pace of development varied from place to place within Geto-Dacian territory. The proof of uninterrupted ethnocultural continuity is provided by the fact that local cultural unity was re-established on a number of occasions (in the 4th-5th, 6th-7th and 8th centuries), that the Romanian language has no dialects, and that the consciousness of belonging to the Roman or Romance world has persisted into our own day, along with traditions inherited from the remote past. By comparison of the archaeological evidence from the former province of Dacia — which has become available on a increasing scale in recent years — with material from the territory of the free Dacians, and the study of Dacian material dating from after 106 A.D., found either in rural areas or on Roman military sites (not only in the *canabae* but even in the *castra* themselves), the problems of continuity, romanisation and unity have been finally resolved.

As we have seen from the discussion in Chapter VII and the accompanying illustrations, the archaeology of the Early Christian period has been considerably enriched in the last few decades by the material discovered throughout Daco-Romania, and not merely in the former Roman province. For the Daco-Romans and Proto-Romanians the new faith became a factor in the development of civilisation which was to extend its impact to other peoples during the mediaeval period. Of particular significance is the popular character and the Latin form which Christianity assumed in Daco-Romania, enriching the fundamental vocabulary with Romano-Latin terms. Thus Christianity played an important historical rôle during the period when the Romanian people was developing and crystallising into its definitive form. It helped to fortify the Roman or Romance culture of the indigenous population by bringing them together in organisations of their own and thus establishing a distinction between them and the migrant peoples. As in western Europe and elsewhere in the Roman Empire, Christianity seems to have established itself first in the towns and later in the country areas. Significant in this respect is the 4th century Christian basilica found by M. Davidescu at Drobeta, the earliest so far discovered in Daco-Romania. By the 7th century even fibulas belonging to the Proto-Romanians were decorated with the symbol of the cross, like the one found at Fărcaşele in the district of Olt.

The exodus from the towns — all of which had been abandoned by the 5th century — to the villages is reflected not only in the spread of Christianity and the use of certain Christian terms taken from an urban setting (like the Romanian *biserică*, " church ", from *basilica*) but also in the application to village life of words derived from the pattern of life in towns (e.g. *pămînt*, " land ", from *pavimentum*).

In spite of the disturbances caused by the repeated passage of migrant peoples the indigenous population remained, in Iorga's phrase, " masters of the land " in Daco-Romania, firmly attached to that land and protected from extermination because they were necessary to the migrants.

Accepting the validity of the theory of "population nappes", we have extended it to other peoples as well as the Slavs, since the archaeological evidence shows that these intrusive layers superimposed on the indigenous population are found in many areas and many periods, varying in frequency, extent and ethnic homogeneity. The one fixed and durable element is the underlying indigenous stock. As we have seen, the Slav nappe extended widely from the Carpathians to Greece. In Daco-Romania it was eliminated and the Slavs were assimilated; but, as in earlier times and again after the 8th-9th centuries, scattered ethnic groups of non-Romance origin survived here and there, sometimes persisting even after the formation of the Romanian people. On the basis of this fact, which is attested also by archaeological evidence, we have advanced the theory of centres of polarisation : i.e. the persistence of the separate communities which are referred to in the written sources as living alongside the Romanians, then long since established as a separate people.

The existence of separate communities among the Geto-Dacians and the Daco-Romans is not subject to doubt. It was the grouping of such communities that gave rise to the *romaniae* and *vlahii* discussed in an earlier chapter ; and when these groups of communities were brought together in a larger structure covering a particular geographical area they produced the territorial units which are referred to in the earliest sources as "lands" (Romanian *ţară*, from Latin *terra*) : the Land of Haţeg, the Land of Făgăraş, the Land of Bîrsa, the Land of Litovoi (Litva), the Land of Maramureş (an area to which Roman rule never extended but where the free Dacians themselves were romanised).

The conclusion that emerges from this study, based on the archaeological evidence, is clear. Within the framework of Daco-Romania the Romanian people came into being on the same territory which they occupy today ; and from time immemorial this region, protected and consolidated by the spinal column of the Carpathians, has developed with unbroken continuity and in perfect unity.

170

A

The free Dacians in the regions bordering the Roman province of Dacia : finds of coins.

B

Diffusion of cultures of the Thracian Bronze Age (2nd millennium B.C.) in Romania.

C

Diffusion of Byzantine coins in Romania in the 6th-7th centuries A.D. and the 8th-13th centuries. After C. Preda ; information added for 1972, 1973 and 1974.

D

Economic relationships of the Geto-Dacians with the southern Greeks before the Roman conquest.

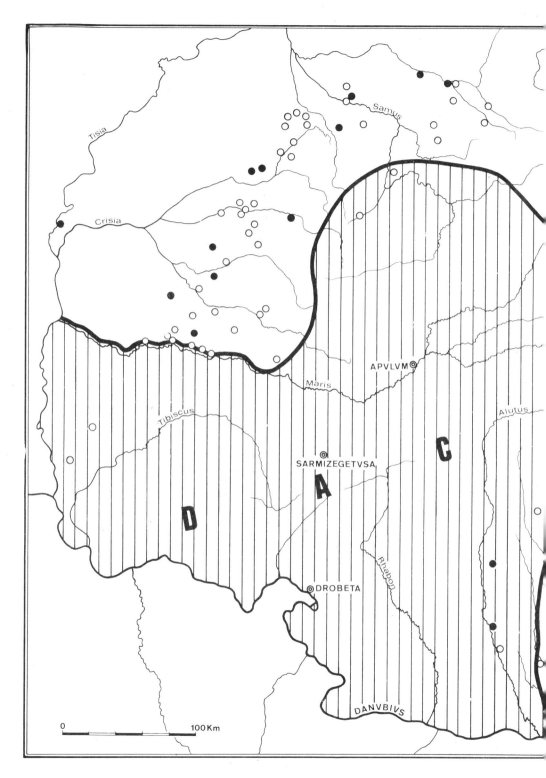

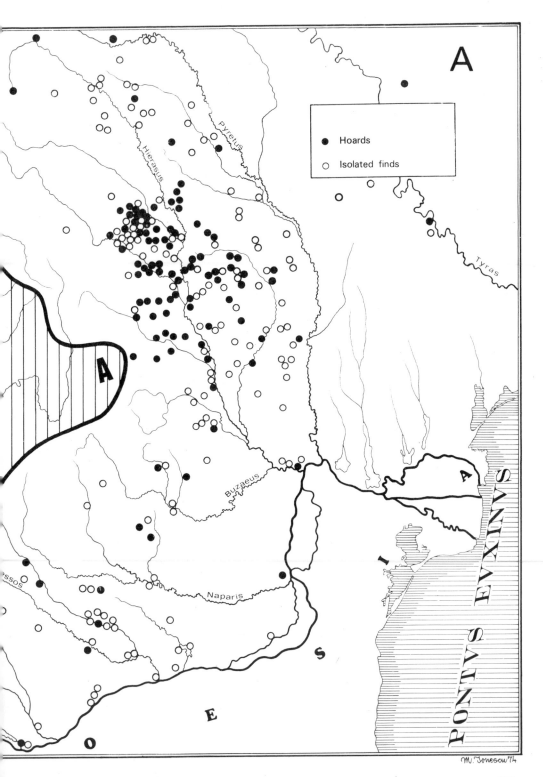

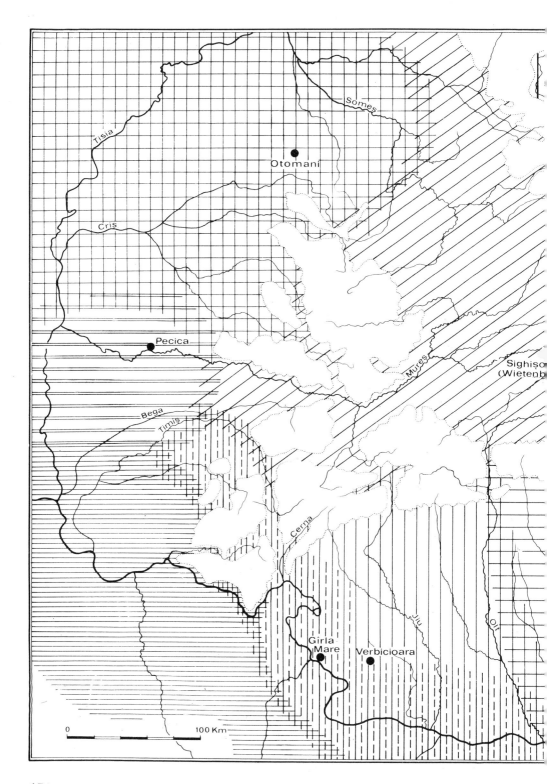

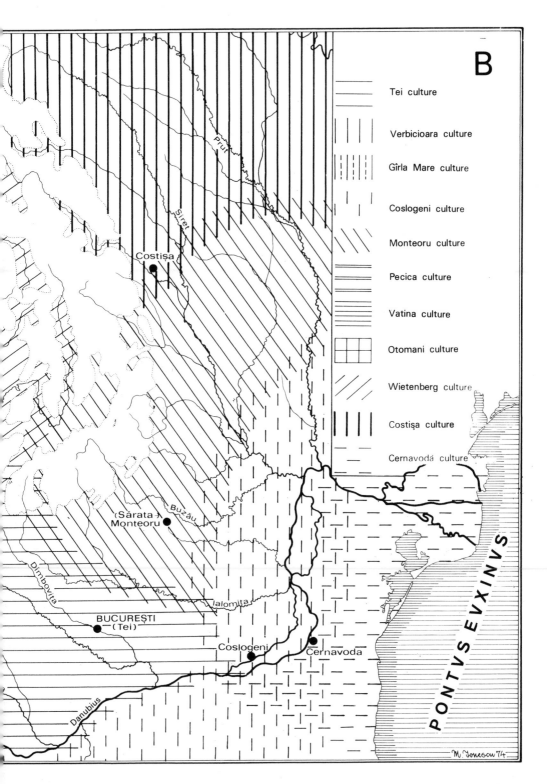

B

	Tei culture
	Verbicioara culture
	Gîrla Mare culture
	Coslogeni culture
	Monteoru culture
	Pecica culture
	Vatina culture
	Otomani culture
	Wietenberg culture
	Costişa culture
	Cernavodă culture

Prut

Siret

Costişa

Buzău

(Sărata)
Monteoru

Dîmbovița

Ialomița

BUCUREŞTI
(Tei)

Coslogeni

Cernavoda

Danubius

PONTVS EVXINVS

M. Ionescu 74

175

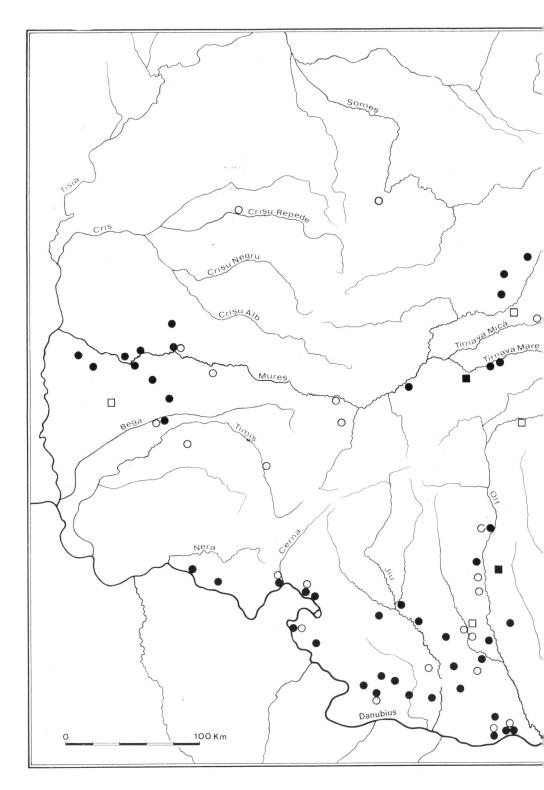

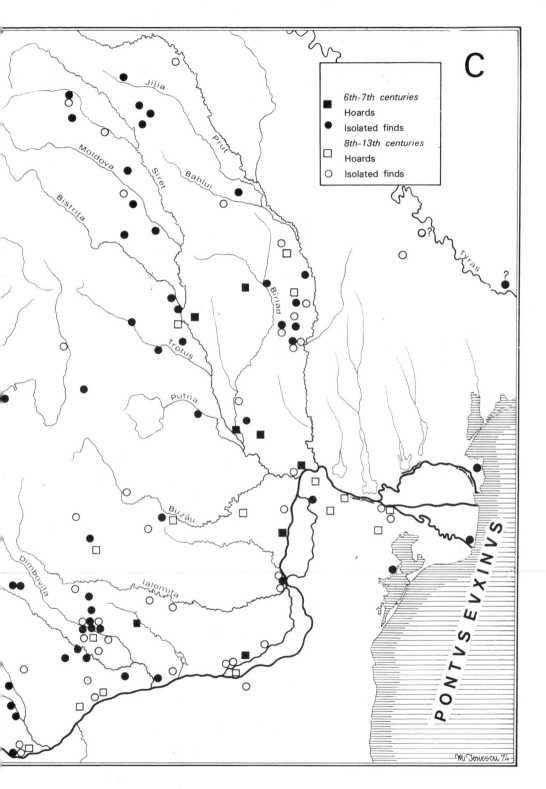

C

6th-7th centuries
■ Hoards
● Isolated finds

8th-13th centuries
□ Hoards
○ Isolated finds

Jijia

Prut

Moldova

Siret

Bahlui

Bistrița

Bîrlad

Trotuș

Putna

Buzău

Dîmbovița

Ialomița

Tyras

PONTVS EVXINVS

M. Ionescu 74

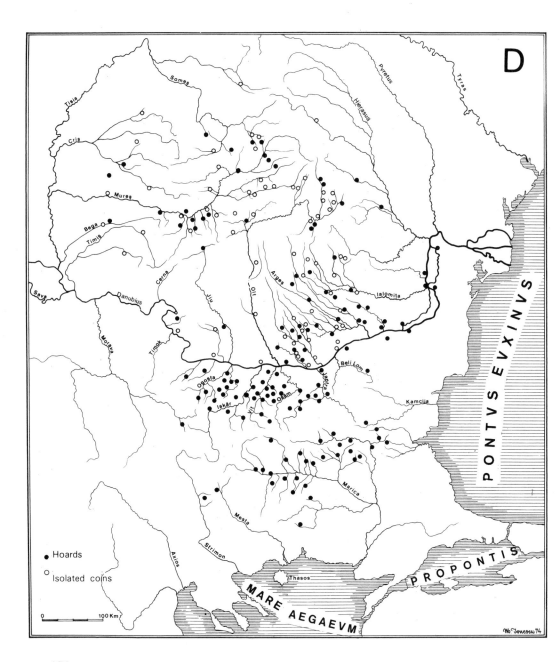

BIBLIOGRAPHY

A. ARMBRUSTER, *Romanitatea românilor* (The Romanity of the Romanians), Bucharest, 1972.

M. BABEŞ, " Dacii şi Bastarnii " (The Dacians and the Bastarnae), *Carpica*, II, 1970.

J. BARNEA and Ş. ŞTEFĂNESCU, *Din istoria Dobrogei* (On the History of the Dobrudja), Vol. II, Bucharest, 1971.

D. BERCIU, *Romania before Burebista* (Ancient Peoples and Places), London, 1967.

D. BERCIU, *Das thrako-getische Fürstengrab von Agighiol in Rumänien.*

D. BERCIU, *Quelques éléments de la civilisation géto-dace et daco-romaine à la lumière des nouvelles recherches archéologiques et leur signification historique*, Bucharest, 1971.

D. BERCIU, *Romanitatea poporului român, în lumina recentelor cercetări arheologice* (The Romanity of the Romanian People in the Light of Recent Archaeological Research), Rîmnicul Vîlcea, 1972.

D. BERCIU, *Contributions à l'art thraco-gète*, Bucharest, 1974.

G. BICHIR, *Cultura Carpică* (The Culture of the Carpi), Bucharest, 1973.

L. BÎRZU, *Continuitatea populaţiei autohtone în Transilvania în sec. IV-V (Cimitirul I de la Bratei)* (The Continuity of the Autochthonous Population in Transylvania in the 4th-5th Centuries : Cemetery No. 1 at Bratei), Bucharest, 1973.

M. CONSTANTINESCU, " Despre formaţiunea social-economică tributală " (On the tributary socio-economic formation), *Memoria Oeconomica*, XXVIII, 1973.

M. COMŞA, " Sur la romanisation des territoires nord-danubiens aux IIIe-VIe siècles de n.è. ", *Nouvelles Etudes d'Histoire*, III, Bucharest, 1965.

H.I. CRIŞAN, *Ceramica daco-getică (cu privire specială la Transilvania)* (Daco-Getic Pottery, with Special Reference to Transylvania), Bucharest, 1969.

H. DAICOVICIU, *Dacia de la Burebista la cucerirea romană* (Dacia from Burebista to the Roman Conquest), Cluj, 1972.

G.T. DAN, " Unele probleme privind evoluţia culturii materiale din Moldova în sec. VI-X " (Some problems concerning the evolution of the material culture of Moldavia in the 6th-10th centuries), *Carpica*, II, 1969.

G.T. DAN, " Regiunile răsăritene ale României în sec. VI-VII " (The eastern regions of Romania in the 6th-7th centuries), *Memoria Antiquitatis*, I, 1969.

G. DIACONU, *Tîrgşor : necropolă din sec. III-IV e.n.* (Tîrgsor : a Necropolis of the 3rd-4th Centuries A.D.), Bucharest, 1965.

G. DIACONU, *Mogoşeni : necropolă din sec. IV e.n.* (Mogoşeni : a Necropolis of the 4th Century A.D.), Tîrgovişte, 1970.

P. DIACONU, *Les Petchénègues dans la région du Bas-Danube*, Bucharest, 1970.

P. DIACONU, *Păcuiul lui Soare —cetatea bizantină* (Păcuiul lui Soare— a Byzantine Citadel). Vol. I, 1972.

S. DUMITRAŞCU, " Aşezări si descoperiri dacice din vestul şi nord-vestul României în sec. II-IV e.n. " (Dacian Settlements and Discoveries in Western and North-Western Romania in the 2nd-4th Centuries A.D.), *Oradea Pedagogic Institute, Scientific Transactions*, 2, 1968.

R. FLORESCU, *Adamclisi*, Bucharest, 1973.

C.C. GIURESCU, *Formarea poporului român* (The Formation of the Romanian People), Bucharest, 1973.

C.C. GIURESCU, "Le jugement par les conjurateurs dans les pays roumains", *Xenion* (Festschrift for Pan J. Zepes), Athens-Freiburg-Cologne, 1973.

L. IONITA, "Elemente autohtone în cultura Sîntana de Mureş din Moldova" (Autochthonous elements in the Sîntana de Mureş culture in Moldavia), *Carpica*, IV, 1971.

A. LÁSZLÓ, "Începuturile metalurgiei fierului pe teritoriul României" (The beginnings of iron metallurgy on the territory of Romania), *SCIVA*, Bucharest, 1974.

M. MACREA, *Viaţa in Dacia romană* (Life in Roman Dacia), Bucharest, 1969.

B. MITREA, "Penetrazione commerciale e circolazione monetaria nella Dacia prima della conquista", *Ephemeris Dacoromana*, X, 1945.

B. MITREA, "Unele probleme în legătură cu necropola prefeudală de la Izvoru-Giurgiu" (Some problems concerning the pre-feudal necropolis of Izvoru-Giurgiu), *SCIV*, 18, 3, Bucharest, 1967.

B. MITREA, "Unitatea geto-dacă reflectată în monetăria dacă" (Geto-Dacian unity reflected in Dacian coins), *Annals of the University of Bucharest, History,* XVIII, 1969.

P.P. PANAITESCU, *Introducere la istoria culturii româneşti* (Introduction to the History of Romanian Culture), Bucharest, 1969.

S. PAPACOSTEA, "Les Roumains et la conscience de leur romanité au Moyen-Age", *Revue Roumaine d'Histoire*, 1965.

R. POPA, *Ţara Maramureşului in veacul al XIV-lea* (The Maramureş Country in the 14th Century), Bucharest, 1970.

C. PREDA, "Circulaţia monedelor bizantine în regiunea carpato-dunăreană" (The circulation of Byzantine coins in the Carpatho-Danubian region), *SCIV*, 23, 3, Bucharest, 1972.

C. PREDA, *Monedele geto-dacilor* (Geto-Dacian Coins), Bucharest, 1973.

C. PREDA and H. NUBA, *Histria III : descoperirile monetare 1914-1970* (Histria III : Finds of Coins 1914-1970), Bucharest, 1973.

F. PREDA, " Procesul pătrunderii mărfurilor greceşti şi consecinţele acestuia în Dacia extracarpatică " (The process of penetration of goods and its consequences in extra-Carpathian Dacia), *Apulum*, XI, Alba Iulia, 1973.

D. PROTASE, *Problema continuităţii în Dacia în lumina arheologiei şi numismaticiei* (The Problem of Continuity in Dacia in the Light of Archaeology and Numismatics), Bucharest, 1966.

I.I. RUSSU, *Limba trace-dacilor* (The Language of the Thraco-Dacians), Bucharest, 1967.

M. RUSU, *Metalurgia bronzului în Transilvania la începutul Hallstattului* (Bronze Metallurgy in Transylvania at the Beginning of the Hallstatt Period) (résumé of doctoral thesis), Cluj, 1972.

G. ŞTEFAN, *Formarea poporului român şi limbii sale* (The Formation of the Romanian People and their Language), Bucharest, 1973.

Ş. ŞTEFĂNESCU, " Les concentrations démographiques et leur signification historique ", *Annales de Démographie Historique,* 1971.

V. TEODORESCU, " La civilisation Ipoteşti-Cîndeşti (V^e-VIIe siècles) ", *Actes du VIIe Congrès international des sciences préhistoriques et protohistoriques, Prague, 21-27 août 1966,* 1971, Vol. II.

O. TOROPU, *Oltenia în secolele IV-X în lumina arheologiei şi numismaticiei* (Oltenia in the 4th-10th Centuries in the Light of Archaeology and Numismatics) (résumé of doctoral thesis), Bucharest, 1944.

D. TUDOR, " Preuves archéologiques attestant la continuité de la domination romaine au nord du Danube après l'abandon de la Dacie sous Aurélien (IIIe-Ve siècles) ", *Dacoromania*, I, Freiburg-Munich, 1973.

R. VULPE and I. BARNEA, *Din istoria Dobrugei*, II, *Romanii la Dunărea de Jos* (On the History of the Dobrudja, II, The Romans on the Lower Danube), Bucharest, 1968.

I. WINKLER, " Schatzfunde römischer Silbermünzen in Dakien bis zum Beginn der Dakerkriege ", *Jahrbuch für Numismatik und Geldgeschichte*, 16, 1966.

V. ZIRRA, *Necropola celtică de la Ciumeşti şi consideraţii cu privire la cunoaşterea Latène-ului* (The Celtic Necropolis at Ciumeşti and Considerations on La Tène Culture) (résumé of doctoral thesis), Bucharest, 1970.

LIST OF ILLUSTRATIONS

20 Gold object from a hoard found in a jar at Ostrovul Mare (Mehedinţi). Gîrla Mare culture. Romanian Historical Museum.

21 Gold bracelet from Transylvania. Last phase of Bronze Age. Romanian Historical Museum.

22 Gold " diadem " from Galeşu (Constanţa). Early Iron Age. Romanian Historical Museum.

23 Gold objects from Şmig (Transylvania). Romanian Historical Museum.

24 Gold treasure from Turnu-Măgurele. Late Bronze Age. Romanian Historical Museum.

25 Gold helmet from Poiana-Coţofeneşti (Prahova) : right-hand cheek-piece and rear peak. Thraco-Getic art, showing Persian influence. First half of 4th century B.C. Romanian Historical Museum.

26 Gold bracelets with spiral ends. From Sacoşul Mare (Transylvania). Last phase of Thracian Bronze Age. Romanian Historical Museum.

27 Lunette-shaped fibula and two horse trappings from the district of Alba. Early Iron Age. Alba Iulia Museum.

28 Thracian arm-protector from deposit at Ighiu (Alba). Bronze Age. Alba Iulia Museum.

29 Socketed axe from the large Drajna de Jos hoard. Romanian Historical Museum.

30 Bronze sickle from the Drajna de Jos hoard.

31 Thracian bronze battle-axe decorated with geometric motifs, with mushroom-shaped butt. From the Apa hoard (Transylvania). Romanian Historical Museum.

32 Bronze hairpin with decorated rhomboid plaque from Medgidia. Noua culture (period of transition from Bronze Age to early Iron Age). Romanian Historical Museum.

33 Single-handled vase with vertical stud and decoration of narrow bands of hatching. Noua culture. Romanian Historical Museum.

34 See No. 31.

35 Large vase with decoration of bands of hatching, triangles and vertical studs. Suciu de Sus culture, also found in north-eastern Hungary. End of Bronze Age and period of transition to early Iron Age (Hallstatt). Romanian Historical Museum.

36 Big-bellied vase with cylindrical neck ; under the neck, relief decoration in moustache-like patterns. From Poiana (Galaţi). Northern Thracian culture of the early Iron Age. Romanian Historical Museum.

37 Upper part of the Medgidia emblem-sword. Thraco-Getic art (animal style) of the 5th century B.C. Romanian Historical Museum.

38 Silver harness ornament ; bands of lighter colour covered with a very thin coat of gold leaf. From the Craiova treasure. 4th century B.C. Romanian Historical Museum.

39 Harness ornament in the shape of a lion, decorated with transverse bands of hatching and small circles. From the Craiova treasure. Thraco-Getic art, 4th century B.C. Romanian Historical Museum.

40 Silver plaque with animals' heads at the four corners from the Craiova " treasure ". Like the many other similar items in the Craiova deposit (some of them triangular in shape), the piece suggests a rapidly whirling motion. 4th century B.C. Romanian Historical Museum.

41 Applied ornament from a Getic tomb at Găvani (Brăila). 4th century B.C. Brăila Museum.

42 Gold beads in the shape of small amphoras, like those found at Agighiol. First half of 4th century B.C. Romanian Historical Museum.

43 Zoomorphic applied ornament (gold) from the Băiceni treasure (district of Iaşi). 4th century B.C. Romanian Historical Museum.

44 Gold bracelet ending in stags' heads, from the Băiceni treasure. 4th century B.C. Romanian Historical Museum.

45 Silver harness frontal (a griffin) from Agighiol (Tulcea). First half of 4th century B.C. Romanian Historical Museum.

46 Hellenistic gold jewellery from Histria. Romanian Historical Museum.

47 Gold necklace with beads in the shape of small amphoras and rings. From Mangalia. Hellenistic period. Romanian Historical Museum.

48 Dacian bronze mask of the Augustan period, found in 1973 in an underground room in citadel No. 1 at Ocniţa-Ocnele Mari (Vîlcea). Rîmnicu Vîlcea Museum.

49 Bronze helmet from the same tomb. 4th century B.C. Brăila Museum.

50 Dacian footed cup, with painted decoration, from citadel No. 1 at Ocniţa-Ocnele Mari. End of 1st century B.C. Rîmnicu Vîlcea Museum.

51 Small peasant lamp. Hellenistic period. Olteniţa Museum.

52 Silver bracelet with a human face from Coada Malului (Ilfov). The style shows elements of continuity with the Thraco-Getic period. Romanian Historical Museum.

53 Gold vase from Şmig. Romanian Historical Museum.

54 Phalera with representation of a human head from Herăstrău (Bucharest). Romanian Historical Museum.

55 Dacian gold ornament from Mediaş (Sibiu). Romanian Historical Museum.

56 Bronze helmet from a Getic tomb. 1st century B.C. Reproduced by courtesy of A. Vulpe. Romanian Historical Museum.

57 Knobbed bracelet from the citadel of Piatra Craivii. Alba Iulia Museum.

58 Dacian iron vase, gilded, from the Dacian citadel of Bîtca Doamnei (Piatra Neamţ). Piatra Neamţ Museum.

59 Dacian silver bracelet with snake protomes from Coada Malului. Romanian Historical Museum.

60 Iron arrowheads from the Dacian citadel of Piatra Craivii (Alba). Alba Iulia Museum.

61 Iron spurs from the Dacian citadel of Piatra Craivii (Alba). Alba Iulia Museum.

62 Necklace of interwoven silver thread from Coada Malului. Thracian style. Romanian Historical Museum.

63 Iron sabre from Dobolii de Jos (Covasna). The cross-pieces of the hilt (No. 65) are in the form of the beaks of birds of prey, and the guard has two animals decorated with transverse bands of hatching, in the style of Thraco-Getic art. 5th century B.C. Romanian Historical Museum.

64 Imported Hellenistic candelabrum from the Dacian oppidum at Crăsani (Ialomiţa). Romanian Historical Museum.

65 See No. 63.

66 Bronze ring with studs (from harness) found in a Getic warrior tomb of the 4th century B.C. Brăila Museum.

67 Dacian fibula with rhomboid disc decorated with circles, in the Thraco-Getic tradition. From Mediaş (Transylvania). Romanian Historical Museum.

68-69 Silver tetradrachm of the 2nd century B.C. from Macedonia Prima, found in Romania. National Museum of Antiquities, Institute of Archaeology, Bucharest.

70-72 Dacian silver coins imitated from the tetradrachms of Philip II of Macedonia. No. 70 : found in Moldavia. Nos. 71-72 : found south of the Danube.

73-74 Silver tetradrachm from Thasos found in Romania. National Museum of Antiquities, Institute of Archaeology, Bucharest.

75-77 See Nos. 70-72. No. 75 : found in Moldavia. Nos. 76-77 : found south of the Danube.

78 Single-handled vase showing native Dacian influence, found in a Celtic context. Romanian Historical Museum.

79 Hand-modelled single-handled vase from the Getic citadel at Stînceşti (Botoşani). 4th century B.C. Romanian Historical Museum.

80 Sherd found at Ocniţa, with the personal name REB written in Roman capitals. 1st century B.C. Romanian Historical Museum.

81-82 Two sherds found at Ocniţa, with writing in the Greek alphabet. 1st century B.C. Rîmnicu Vîlcea Museum.

83 Wax tablet from Dacia. Romanian Historical Museum.

84 Roman sarcophagus from Romula. Romanian Historical Museum.

85 Roman *terra sigillata*. Romanian Historical Museum.

86 Small hand-modelled peasant lamp of typically Dacian type, from Ocniţa. Rîmnicu Vîlcea Museum.

87 Brick with the stamp (reversed) of Legio XIII Gemina. Romanian Historical Museum.

88 Small Roman peasant lamp. Romanian Historical Museum.

89 Dacian applied ornament with horseman, from Ciurcea (Covasna). Romanian Historical Museum.

90 Dacian silver knobbed fibula from Mediaş (Braşov). 1st century A.D. Romanian Historical Museum.

91 Phalera from Ciurcea, showing continuity with the Thraco-Getic period. 1st century B.C. Romanian Historical Museum.

92-93 Roman silver vases from Muncelu de Sus (Iaşi). Beginning of 2nd century A.D. By courtesy of Ion Mitrea and V. Mihăilescu-Bîrliba. Museum of Archaeology, Piatra Neamţ.

94 Roman sculpture from Apulum. Alba Iulia Museum.

95 Female bust from Apulum. 2nd-3rd century A.D. Alba Iulia Museum.

96 Statuette of the god Osiris, found in the Banat. Roman period. Timişoara Museum.

97 Roman lead weight from Tomis. Romanian Historical Museum.

98 Figure of Dionysos from the Banat. 2nd-3rd century A.D. Timişoara Museum.

99 Roman funerary medallion from Aiud. Roman provincial style. 2nd century A.D. Romanian Historical Museum.

100 Funerary stele from Alburnus Maior, showing local features. Romanian Historical Museum.

101 Funerary stele of Tiberius Claudius Maximus, with representation of the death of Decebal, from Grammeni (Philippi). 2nd century A.D. Kavalla Museum.

102 Funerary column from Apulum referring to a native Dacian named Mucapor, son of Mucatra. 3rd century A.D. Romanian Historical Museum.

103 Roman funerary medallion from Transylvania, showing local features. 3rd century A.D. Romanian Historical Museum.

104 Roman pottery rhyton of the 2nd-3rd century A.D. Romanian Historical Museum.

105 Roman mould for terra sigillata. Romanian Historical Museum.

106 See No. 101.

107 Thracian horseman from Tirighina-Barboşi (Galaţi). 2nd-3rd century A.D. Galaţi Museum.

108 Funerary stele from Căşei (Transylvania). Local art. 3rd century A.D. Romanian Historical Museum.

109 Daco-Roman urn from Soporu de Cîmpie. Romanian Historical Museum.

110 Mithraic monument from Romula, in three registers. 3rd century A.D. Romanian Historical Museum.

111-112 Gold treasure ("Closca cu Pui") of Pietroasele (Buzău). Romanian Historical Museum. Late 4th - early 5th century.

113 Bronze statuette of a Lar from Sucidava. 2nd-3rd century A.D. Romanian Historical Museum.

114-117 Treasure of gold objects from Pietroasele (Buzău). Late 4th-early 5th century A.D. Romanian Historical Museum.

118 Gold necklace from Apahida II treasure. Romanian Historical Museum.

119-121 Gold jewellery and belt buckle from Someşeni (Cluj), of types similar to those found in the Apahida treasures. 5th century A.D. Romanian Historical Museum.

122 a and b. Treasure of Bălăciţa (Mehedinţi). 3rd century A.D. Drobeta Museum, Turnu Severin.

123 Silver-gilt pitcher from the treasure of Tăuteni (Bihor). 5th century A.D. Oradea Museum.

124 Pitcher from the Tăuteni treasure. 5th century A.D. Oradea Museum.

125 Digitated fibula of Avar type. Romanian Historical Museum.

126 Digitated fibula from Breheni (Olt). 7th century A.D. Slatina Museum.

127 Vase from the Sînnicolau Mare treasure.

128 Small Early Christian bronze lamp of peasant type from Luciu (Ialomiţa). 6th century A.D. Romanian Historical Museum.

129 Byzantine gold coin with effigies of the Emperor Heraclius and his son, found in an Avar tomb at Sînpetru German (Arad). 7th century A.D. Arad Museum.

130 Daco-Roman vase with band of pecked ornament from Moigrad (Transylvania). Romanian Historical Museum.

131 Pottery vessel from Capidava (Constanţa), with the Romanian word *Petre* inscribed on it. 10th century A.D. Romanian Historical Museum.

132 Single-handled pot, showing native influence, from 4th century inhumation cemetery at Oinac-Giurgiu. Sîntana de Mureş culture. Giurgiu Museum.

133 Lamp, with lid, from Obreja (Sibiu). Dacian workmanship. Romanian Historical Museum.

134 Wheel-turned vase from the Geto-Roman cemetery at Enisala. Romanian Historical Museum.

135 Cemetery at Soporu de Cîmpie (Sibiu). Daco-Roman. Romanian Historical Museum.

136 Large three-handled grey pot, wheel-turned, from cemetery at Oinac-Giurgiu. Sîntana de Mureş culture. 4th century A.D. Giurgiu Museum.

137 Christian symbol in the form of a fish, with a cross on one side and the monogram of Christ on the other, from Luciu. 6th century A.D. Romanian Historical Museum.

138 Detail of No. 123 : Muse with mask and thyrsus.

INDEX

Finished in october 1978.
Printed on the presses of Nagel publishers in Geneva.
Binding by Nagel.
Legal deposit Nr 720.
Printed in Switzerland.

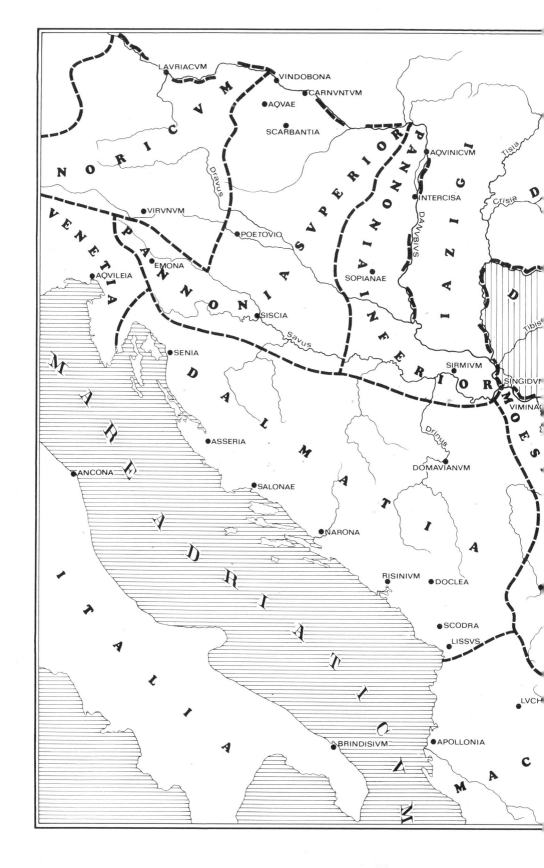